Everything Is Your Fault

Changing your life with responsibility, leadership, and meditation

Everything Is Your Fault

Changing your life with responsibility,
leadership, and meditation

Rajan Shankara

BOOKS

Winchester, UK
Washington, USA

JOHN HUNT PUBLISHING

First published by O-Books, 2021
O-Books is an imprint of John Hunt Publishing Ltd., 3 East St., Alresford,
Hampshire SO24 9EE, UK
office@jhpbooks.com
www.johnhuntpublishing.com
www.o-books.com

For distributor details and how to order please visit the 'Ordering' section on our website.

Design: Stuart Davies

UK: Printed and bound by CPI Group (UK) Ltd, Croydon, CR0 4YY
Printed in North America by CPI GPS partners

We operate a distinctive and ethical publishing philosophy in
all areas of our business, from our global network of authors to
production and worldwide distribution.

Contents

A special thanks to my parents for being philosophers, activists, and writers. To the monks for sharpening my mind in the fires of discipline. To my two sisters for paving the way and exploring the world first. Thank you to all the people who stopped to speak to me, teach me, and show me the way when I was lost, confused, and needing answers.

Thank you, Bodhinatha
Aum Namasivaya

Introduction

The trunk of my car was full of marijuana, some light weapons and cocaine as I was being pulled over by a cop on a quiet Indiana road while driving back from Chicago on a supply run in my 1990 Honda Accord. I had never been pulled over on a supply run before and I'd never been stopped by a K-9 unit. My mind went blank as I turned off the car and I immediately took responsibility for what was going to happen—my life was over. I was going to jail, and it was all my fault. Nevertheless, a mysterious calm swept over me and I was ready to face the situation with pure focus and attention. The officer—about my height and in his fifties, solid build, in shape and well shaven—walked up to the window and shined his flashlight around the dashboard and then at me.

"Do you realize that your windows are tinted way too dark?" the officer said as he looked at me puzzled, wondering if the law meant anything to me at all. I lied and said, "Ah, nope, thought Indiana tolerated the tints. Sorry about that, officer," knowing full well that the windows were beyond legal.

"Step out of the car," he said.

"Yes, sir," came out my mouth with full confidence. *What did it matter anyway?* In that moment I was already dead.

As I was getting out, he asked that I walk behind the car over to the trunk, which I did. I turned around and he was facing me, and I was facing right back at him.

"Do you mind if I search your trunk?"

"No, sir, I don't mind at all."

It was about this time that I noticed the barking dog in the backseat of the police car and it hit me that I was pulled over by a K-9 unit. I looked over but couldn't see the dog, only the grey steel caging separating the world from that furious animal. The cop noticed that I looked back at his dog and joined me in the motion by turning his head and flashlight at the back seat of his patrol car and then turning back to me. With a sly sneaky smirk on his face the officer asked, "Do you mind if *he* searches too? Oh and can I search you?" Always a trick question in this kind of situation. If I say no then I look guilty, but saying yes opens me up to the possibility of being exposed.

"No, sir, I don't mind at all," was the only thing that came out. I stared him right in the eye and waited for my future to end. We locked eyes for what seemed like 30 long seconds until he turned off his flashlight, put it back in its holster, and said three words I will never forget:

"I trust you."

Making a swift motion to his radio he lowered the volume and walked back to his car, turned around, and drove back into the quiet night from which he came. I stood there motionless. I looked at the car, my feet on top of the solid asphalt, and the whole area around me in disbelief—quiet and still. It was as if the town and everything else inside it didn't exist. I was alone but I was also free.

My heartbeat slowly caught up with my breath and my hands stopped quivering after a few minutes of resting on the trunk. It was then that I made a vow to correct my path. I decided to never break the law again and live the most honorable life I could. I knew I was given a second chance and I was going to make the most of it. The next day I peeled the tints off my windows, gave the drugs away to another dealer, fixed my thug perspective on life, and looked at the world with a fresh pair of eyes—as if I was looking at life clearly for the first time.

* * *

… Fast forward some 15 years later and I've become an accomplished monk, meditation guide, personal trainer, writer (albeit not a good one), mentor, business owner, stress reliever and mountain biker. A lot has changed since that night with the police officer. I made a vow to change my life and give back to society, and I did. The book that unfolds is the story of my life with specific focus given to the age of 15 to 32. From a no-good youth drug dealer; to business owner; to a 12-year-life as a monk; I've seen and done a lot and I've tried to not only sum it up in one book, but also in one sentence: Everything is Your Fault.

Section 1: Ownership, Responsibility and Suffering

Everything is your fault

Well, not everything can possibly be your fault. The starving, jobless, ill, and the insane people of the world are not your fault. Cardi B is not your fault and neither is the latest reality TV show… but everything else is. Everything that goes on inside your mind and your reactions to life itself is made up of your decisions. The world outside you is not in your control but the internal response to that world is, and to consciously choose is your greatest power in life. In between stimulus and response is a moment in which we can either act with wisdom or emotion. It is our response to stimulus that shows what we're made of. It shows our character, our personality, and most importantly it shows what we do when given the opportunity to act. Choose wisely.

Here's a philosophical bit of information: There's nothing inherently good, bad, right, or wrong about what goes on around us—things are just the way they are and nothing in life has or will ever inform you, "I am this or that." The fallen pot of boiling water, the broken glass all over the floor, your car running out of gas, and even your cheating spouse will never declare and decide how it should make you feel. Yet, throughout our entire life there is one decider who remains, who is always present and accounted for, and who is always available to judge the situation. That judge is you. We apply our own qualifiers to every situation. That means we add qualities and structure-building-concepts around whatever happens to us. Some *thing* is going to make you feel this or that emotion and it never ends because that is how our mind attempts to stay sane. The mind only understands concrete structure in order to categorize and catalogue life events. It's when the abstract, the unknown, and the unexplored anomaly of life happens that we get lost, confused, depressed, anxiety-ridden, and hopeless.

Having control over our own judgments in life is a power and skill that we are born with but never nurture enough to utilize its full capacity. We get true sanity when we start taking responsibility for situations, people, and things that involve us. With responsibility we can take ownership, with ownership we can fix and repair a broken situation or prevent anything from breaking in the first place. Try, for once in your life, to take the burden of living on yourself and explore the possibility of relieving others of their pain as we relieve our own.

The ability to relieve pain is the greatest skill anyone can have. Not only must we solve our own problems, but once accomplished, we can then become responsible for the pain that others endure on a daily basis. This is the nature of relationships—work or personal—and it is extremely valuable in an ever-expanding global society. To share, support, give back, and withhold our own need for gratification eventually makes us the effective and powerful person we were born to be.

* * *

The aphorisms in this book are meant to be daily reflections. The whole book isn't meant to be read at once, and you don't need to memorize every aphorism as if it's a rule. Some of the aphorisms are meant for you and others won't apply to your life at all. Or, perhaps they all apply. My intentions are not to directly advise and inform you on exactly what to do or how to be. Instead, I'd like to provoke thought and get you thinking. Critical thinking is a way to observe—and manage—personal trauma and confusion. It is an exploratory process that everyone needs to have in order to live the life they want.

The work herein is an expression of my life and I still don't understand how it all happens to work day to day. Looking back I'm amazed to be alive, healthy, free, and simple. I wasn't always headed down a good path. In fact, most of my youth was spent hurting others, making money from selling drugs, and having the mentality of a no-good loser thug that wanted to make others afraid at the very sight of me. I was a misguided youth that appeared untrainable. A lost soul with little hope.

Of course, my life started out normal like most do but over time my outlook changed drastically, taking me from normal youth to criminally active. Thank God I was given a second chance. With that second chance, I went from being a teenager owning his own business to a robed monk living a life of selfless service in the jungles of Hawaii. Now, somehow, I'm a civilian again and trying to help others. It's my hope that I can be a good example of what a man ought to be and to teach others about their own innate peace, their own ability to take responsibility for their thoughts and actions, and to live the glorious life they were meant to have—so long as they realize that everything is their fault.

In the middle of writing my autobiography an opportunity to go to Santa Fe, New Mexico presented itself. While walking up Canyon Road, a street famous for art galleries, I stopped at a little teahouse for a respite from the New Mexico sun. It was in this little teahouse that I decided to write a different style of book. I would blend my autobiography along with meditative and reflective aphorisms that have been a part of my mind for several years. As you read I will give accounts of my life experiences and the lessons obtained. And I'll try to make this as short as possible so we can all get on with our day. I've separated the aphorisms and reflective paragraphs with three * * * so you know I've transitioned to the autobiographical portion of the text.

My work revolves around helping others in their search for becoming effective and powerful people. A person undaunted by anomaly, unchanged by circumstances, constantly aware and in charge of any given situation. Becoming the best version of myself, mastering the mind and understanding my relationships, revolves around consistency and unwavering resolve to move forward no matter what. We live as coddled humans in a world of constant technological change, and it's natural to seek pleasure and comfort. However, I've found that most things that change our lives for the better are hard, unpleasant, and uncomfortable. For ultimate transformation we need friction. Friction creates heat and enough heat can melt steel. And so it is with our character, our personality and our mindset. Once we understand that changing our nature requires the heat of experience in order to alter our state, we can then begin to treat what goes on in our life with respect, as if something sacred is happening, as if every pain and suffering is our greatest teacher.

We are the cause of all our suffering

Everything comes from us. Our joy, sorrow, happiness, sadness, confusion, mistakes, and success. Everything we experience or perceive, both mentally and emotionally, passes through a self-guided filtration system inside the mind. These filters are innate and conditioned by our past *and current* ways of thinking. They are the five filters of the mind: Conscious, Subconscious, Sub of the Subconscious, Superconscious or Intuitive, Sub-superconscious, and will be covered later in this book. We create our present moment by what we've learned and said in the past, and by what we've been told. We then let that shape who we *think* we are. We are our own creation, the good and the bad.

If it didn't come from our own manifestation then we allowed society to shape us through what's called the social mirror. Author and speaker, Stephen Covey, tells about his philosophy of the social mirror in his work *The 7 Habits of Highly Effective People*. He defines the social mirror as a projection of the world's influences on us. The social mirror is not an invention we create on our own, and it should be observed as well as carefully curated and checked for inconsistencies. At some point, over the course of our lives, we have all been misguided. We have been told who we are by the people around us. These people may have been parents, teachers, siblings, friends, neighbors, role models, actors, coworkers, etc... Whether knowingly or unknowingly, we may have been influenced by some or all of these people in our lives. It may contain invalid data from anecdotal assessments that others have made of their situation brought on by their own reactions. Essentially, this type of projection from other people's insecurities, failures, disappointments or successes, and life experience is everyone else's expansion or limitation of form and action—it's their story, not yours. Form can be defined as a person's mental abilities, capacities and concepts—their conditioning—while action can be understood as a person's response—physical and verbal—to the world around him/her.

You may have done this at one time, too. Perhaps you projected your ideas of success, or your insecurities, fears, regrets, and remorse onto someone else without knowing it. You did it subconsciously. Maybe you've said to someone close to you, "You shouldn't do that. I don't think that's good for you because it's not good for me." Someone close to you will say, "Oh, you can't do that. Ya, I tried already and it didn't work." That may be true for them but not for you. From my experience, I've seen people harm others due to their own self-doubt and low self-esteem. Something they tried didn't work out so they projected onto others their own sense of failure. I've also seen people be affected by someone else's self-doubt and low self-esteem in harmful and hazardous ways. The social mirror can be based on false or irrelevant information and experience, so make sure to pay close attention to what you're being told, and how you're feeling. Sometimes the social mirror may have taken hold and manipulated your own thinking into someone else's experience.

To avoid suffering from the social mirror you must detach from others' thoughts and opinions using your own intuition to guide your life. Detachment is having the ability to release the energy of awareness from objects, situations, or people. Learning to detach may be hard for you at first but I believe anything worthwhile always is. I also firmly believe that my intuition is the voice of my soul and it's important to me to take the time to listen closely and follow that guidance. Intuition reveals itself through direct knowing without study or reflection on a given subject, thought, or idea. When we are in intuition, or in the intuitive part of the mind, we just have a feeling or knowing that something needs to happen a certain way. Meditation is the thread that leads us to our own direct knowing that is intuition. That's how I ended up leaving everything to move to the jungle and study meditation for 12 years.

* * *

> I realized that it was not by wisdom that poets write their
> poetry, but by a kind of nature or inspiration, such as you
> find in seers and prophets; for these also say many beautiful
> things, but do not know anything of what they say.
> Socrates

I will begin by saying I know very little about most things.
What I do know is something my guru taught me long ago: that
the root of all suffering is identification, or attachment, with
situations, people, things—our reality surrounding our daily
lives. Problems arise when people assume that what they are
aware of is closely linked to their real selves. Identifying with
who I used to be is a good place to begin this short story.

I lived in a home with two parents that had three children:
two girls and me. I don't recall all of the details of my early
youth but everything seems like a typical American boyhood
from the stories I've heard and the pictures I've seen—sports,
friends, birthdays, etc. I'm not sure why but most of my pre-teen
memory of myself and others is gone.

My mother, Paulette, came from a lineage of waitresses
who were gone most of the day and night, and didn't have the
resources to properly care for their children. She never revealed
much about her past to me but I did learn that from early on
she was an independent child. She drank coffee before turning
10 and grew up fast due to her circumstances. My grandmother
wasn't around enough so she had to fend for herself, and learn
the ways of the world without much parental guidance. Despite
everything she went through as a child, my mom grew up and
scraped by as a hippie in the infamous Haight-Ashbury District
in California. She became a teacher and taught American and

International Middle-School History, English, and Conflict-Resolution across different grade levels. She married my dad in her mid-twenties and had my two older sisters and me.

When I didn't go to school and was too young to be home alone, I would go to school and sit in on my mother's classes. I always admired watching her work and interact with the students. My mom is very kind, soulful, and direct with people. There's no mask of secrecy or bashfulness. She is direct and in your face and I love that.

My mother is a writer, philosopher, and the leader of her own Wiccan covenant. (Who knew a Wiccan High Priestess would make a Hindu monk?) I get my writing inspiration from having her blood run through my veins, and she led her children to the beliefs of karma, dharma, reincarnation, and inherent divinity in all things. The decision to become a monk was easy, thanks to my mother. It wasn't that much of a surprise to her at all, and I will explain later how my mother gave me the exact piece of advice I needed to get access inside the monastery.

My father, Maurice, was born in Egypt and emigrated to Turkey before coming to America with his mother and father as a young boy. He is a sweet, kind-hearted soul and very hard working. I spent less time overall with my father due to the early divorce of my parents, but still feel like I was able to get close to him even though he didn't seem like he could communicate his feelings all the time. Maurice was a respiratory therapist in Chicago, Illinois for over thirty years and helped people breathe after getting gunshots, serious lung infections, and smoking diseases. The little time we had together as father and son was spent playing catch, throwing a football, or golfing. In the evenings he would make dinner while I did homework and then watch a movie. Breakfast would always be ready when I got up and then it was back to Mom's. I should note here that my father inspired me to start weightlifting, a hobby that would turn into a passion at the age of 16, and then a career later in life. My love of philosophy spawned from my dad as well. He would always be reading an autobiography, biography, or history books. I was encouraged to look over the *Encyclopedia Britannica* when I was waiting for dinner. Back then we didn't have Wikipedia, so I would go over to his giant bookshelves and grab a book by the letter, plop it down on the dining room table, and start going over every single thing in the world that started with the letter "L."

Today, after years of slowly detaching from my family in pursuit of knowledge, I am trying to rebuild my connection with my family. My sisters have kids of their own, growing up before our eyes. My parents are retired and living their own lives — and I'm still seeing where I fit into all of it.

The trouble with my youth began when my parents went through a rough divorce when I was about seven or eight. Being raised by one parent is not ideal and for me that meant growing up without a father figure to guide me into manhood. Instead, I went through my formative years with a mother that was quite separate from my life, and someone who was more of a friend than a figure of leadership.

My life after their divorce was spent playing baseball as an all-star catcher. I was short and stocky enough to crouch for hours, and my throw to second base was fast enough to pick off anyone stealing first. Hockey came after baseball, along with skateboarding all throughout junior high. I started smoking marijuana heavily just before high school and as I entered high school I became a drug dealing bodybuilder in my mother's basement. I left hockey as I went into freshman year of high school because the coaches were assholes, and at the time I would have rather been free on a skateboard than be yelled at for not being fast enough on ice.

Suffering is often prolonged by our attachment to it

We all identify with something. "We" meaning the lens that views reality, our awareness. You could say that the eyes are the lens that views the world, but that which sees the world is beyond the eyes. The term for "that which sees" is awareness, and our awareness likes to think it is what it sees. The mind on the other hand is that which judges what awareness sees, that's what our mind is good at—judging and categorizing.

Sometimes we identify who we are with the help of society—our family and friends, or pop culture—or we identify with where we are from and the culture and traditions that emanate from there. San Francisco is a good example. If you were born and raised in that iconic city then it will be very hard to escape it. Just the idea of San Francisco alone comes with so much rich history. It's as if you were a part of it all by living there. It's human nature to attach our awareness onto a concept of "the tribe" because there's an innate sense of wanting to belong to a group or family. We find our people, or we find our aloneness, and live out that expected reality. Some identify with the pain, suffering, or grief that came along with their childhood. Without pain or hurt some people wouldn't know what else to identify with. A child may cry as a means for getting attention, or an adult may abuse alcohol or narcotics—even attempt to take their own life—for the very same reason as the child. Whether it is our upbringing, our location, or our intimate circle, we all use something as an identification factor when determining who we are and what we are all about.

Once we can look within by turning our lens of awareness around we can then begin to identify with a more permanent identity, or that within us that does not change. This is the process of letting go of our story and grabbing onto our spirit, the force that has been with us from the beginning and will always remain with us, as us. That's why people walk along forest trails, why they mountain bike, surf, meditate, take psychoactive drugs like mushrooms and acid, and jump out of airplanes. There's a mysterious process in which we can let go of attachments and return to the real joy that lay within us. Some do this with extreme sports, which drives them into the present moment like nothing else, or some join a monastery and become monks. The result is the same. We let go of attachments, release suffering momentarily, and return back to who we really are.

* * *

Dealing drugs and lifting weights were my way of being a man when I was a young, misguided teenager. I was completely ignorant to the fact that being a thug was the opposite of manhood. I had no tribe or family community so I created one. I saw myself as the paterfamilias of my own tribe, a tribe that sought to make money from selling pot, mushrooms and cocaine. Gangster rap (as it was known in the 90s) became the inspiration needed to fuel the ridiculous lifestyle of never being sober, not going to class, and trying to make as many people fear us as we could while making money illegally. When a young mind has a lack of leadership it will begin an attempt to lead itself, oftentimes resulting in overuse and abuse of power.

Society used to have teachers, leaders, role models, fathers, and wisemen as a part of the community. In those times we learned from someone older and more experienced than ourselves. That person was able to guide us as we matured. Today we are born into a society that is without community leaders. We have skills but no one to help us develop them. We have strength, but no one to help hone that strength into wise action. Instead, we are taught to be our own master, our own teacher, and our own man or woman. How can a young, inexperienced mind teach itself experience, wisdom, and courage? It has to fail many times in order to understand truth, humility, and courage in facing responsibility head on.

After high school I continued to sell drugs not for the money but for the reputation it gave me. We expanded to the point that we were receiving bricks of pot through the mail system, while making larger and more dangerous deals with Chicago suppliers. Operations had gone so well for so long there wasn't a real need to stop. My mother and I moved to Indiana after I barely graduated high school. Around the same time I was banned from all public facilities in the southside Chicago suburb I grew up in—a defining moment in my "career." Nothing was better for my street credit, and the level of attention I was getting from my small community of friends only made my ego larger. My commute for running drugs increased, and the legality of the situation grew more sensitive. I was crossing into another state with enough drugs to make even more trouble for myself, more risk. But there's no better motivation for a youth craving a dangerous lifestyle than the attention of the police and an increasing list of people on your "do not trust" list—which is everyone other than yourself.

As soon as we take suffering and pain to be our fault, we can begin to take responsibility. We can fix any situation when we are the one to blame.

Making everything our fault is hard, but it has an upside—freedom. Freedom means we have the choice to take responsibility of any situation, and once we are in control of a situation we can either repair it or make sure it never happens in the first place. Who else can fix something for you? Taking blame is not about being a victim, it's about being the leader of every moment. Being responsible allows you to change something instead of placing blame on something else and waiting for a solution to appear. Stop waiting for others. Take the blame. Be responsible. And put yourself and your team where they need to be.

One challenge I've come across regarding this aphorism and the entire book's philosophy as a whole is in relationships. One spouse may try to adjust to the other's faults by taking responsibility and not expressing their true feelings. Keeping a feeling to oneself may in fact be an effective tactic regarding proactivity in the workplace, but when it comes to someone you live with—and especially someone you love—your hidden expression of how you really feel will slowly eat away at you from the inside and will later express itself as an explosion. Letting someone know how you feel is also another way to take blame and responsibility. Speaking out loud for all to hear, including yourself, allows for ideas that have not yet taken form—or taken manifestation—to see the light of day. When a thought stays inside the mind it festers and foments the thinker, you. Our mind is the realm of the abstract, where ideas and concepts don't have to be realistic, practical, or even logical. So, when a thought gets held inside ourselves without release it will appear much mightier than it actually is. A slight worry can evolve into downright fear, destruction, and annihilation if kept within this realm of imagination. However, once a thought from your head leaves the realm of the mind—of the abstract—and goes to the world of form where we can put shapes, colors and words to it, you can finally see and work with a solid structure of form instead of just concepts.

The key to effective communication being a reliable source of harmony in a relationship is to renounce what you've said right after saying it. In other words, it is completely normal to voice your opinion with your spouse but the consequence of voicing your opinion is and will always be the possibility of rejection. You have to express yourself, but forcing your perspective on someone else is simply manipulation, driving people further away. Instead, say what you feel and ask for clarity. Seek to know if your spouse, coworkers, bosses, friends, and family feel the way you do—or let them determine if you are out of line. If you are wrong, how can the conversation go on without resentment or hard feelings? We tend to imagine the worst when an idea is caught inside the mind, but in reality it just needs to be brought out and become known in a more concrete way instead of as a vague idea no one can "see." A thought can do more damage inside your mind than it can outside the mind, and there's nothing worse than living with someone you feel you can't express yourself to or be yourself around.

* * *

Shortly after my second chance I began working at a small warehouse called Louisville Ladder. I learned how to take an invoice for orders of ladders, wrap them up with plastic wrap, and put them in a truck. My proclivity to weightlifting and athletics made the job quite easy as I could lift and haul ladders without stopping. The position was temporary and I was eventually returned to the temp agency that set me up with the job. Next, I was placed in a position with UPS. I was the guy loading boxes onto trucks... and I was terrible at it. I was trying to be good and helpful and all of that, but I was ignorant when it came to working with others. Even worse, I had too much of an ego to be a decent subordinate. Going from being my own boss in a dangerous environment to the apprentice position who had to follow rules was a difficult transition that continued for several years.

In the mornings I was going to Prairie State Community College in Illinois for a career in personal training. Then, I'd drive to Indiana to work in the UPS warehouse. Lifting weights was more than a daily routine at that point, and I began to study exercise science to a degree that could be considered slightly obsessive. My best friend, Tony, eventually rescued me from UPS when he came home from a 3-day work trip in a town about 30 minutes away from where we grew up.

"I've got something for us. It's the real thing," Tony told me when he arrived back at my mom's house from his adventure.

"Oh, ya? What is it?"

"We're going to start our own asphalt maintenance company. This guy Rob is going to let us work to pay off his truck and tank, and we will be on our own." Tony continued to explain the mission, and our discussion lasted into the night. The next chapter of my life began and that week we did, indeed, take over Rob's company. We started out knocking on doors, seeking driveway and parking lot sealcoating gigs—and it worked. It wasn't long, maybe a month, before we got our own apartment in Indiana and worked on the business almost every day. We worked hard because for the first time we actually cared about what we did. Tony and I developed a passion for the quality of our work, to make as much money as we could, and only taking days off when it rained.

Tony took the lead in the operation. He had a natural ability to talk to anyone so he was the first one to knock on doors. He landed the job and when it came time to do the job, he controlled the brush. The brush was where all the finesse came with sealcoating asphalt. The bucketman, me, had to be strong and quick in order to deliver the tar to the brushman and make his job easier. Left and right, the brushman moved the liquid like it was his paint and the ground his canvas.

Day by day we worked harder, got more jobs per day, and eventually landed parking lots at restaurants and law offices. Tony and I learned to sealcoat and stripe in the middle of the night, and be finished in time for the business to open the next morning. We were hungry for it, and all of our energy went towards the business. Not much time passed before our mentor, Rob, got us in touch with asphalt trucks who could deliver fresh asphalt to the job. We started renting steamrollers and laying down new driveways with a small crew of friends. Life was good... or so we thought. We were two young men with their own place and lots of money. Living like this eventually brought me to my knees in misery. It was the catalyst that changed my life forever.

Trust is the highest form of motivation.

Trusting others is the highest form of motivation a leader can offer to their people. When we trust others, we give them air to breathe around us. It gives leaders a chance to let people fail, succeed, explore, discover, and most importantly—room to grow. When leaders clamp down on their team with a vice-like grip it suffocates, alienates, dispels motivation, and lets everyone around them know that there's no way anyone is going to change the current system. Trust empowers people to become better than you and to let that happen takes humility. This process is the very thing that expands team solidarity and success.

Without trust there's insecurity. A leader's ability to trust their people implies that they are good at what they do. But lack of trust, micromanagement, and a constant looking-over-the-shoulder mentality (breathing down necks) is just a person who, deep down, doesn't completely trust themselves. It's not that the other people are personally needing to be watched but more so the leader is unsure of where the goal is and how to effectively get there. A serious lack of communication, or inability to communicate with one's own self, is the root of the issue in every micromanagement situation.

* * *

As a 19-year-old entrepreneur I still had an undeveloped mind without purpose or meaning. I had no understanding of maturity so I didn't know what to do with all the money we were making. It neither made me content nor happy. But what brings contentment? Why are we even alive? What does God want from us? There was a point where I became angry and argumentative with whatever force or being created me. I started to ask big questions and have long philosophical discussions with Tony during and after work. All day we would contemplate the purpose of man's place in the universe as we made our riches. We finally had the means to create wealth, a dream of ours since childhood, but it wasn't enough. I kept thinking there had to be more to life than just money, fun, and girls.

Rain eventually visited the small Indiana town of Valparaiso and work came to a halt for Tony and me, so we did what any teenage boy would do in his apartment, we would read. Tony was good at researching metaphysics online, and one grey and rainy morning he brought a book to my attention.

"Here start reading this with me, you are going to love it," he said as he opened up the digital version of *Autobiography of a Yogi* on the browser. The book, by Paramahansa Yogananda, covers his life and adventures as a Yogi from India making his way to the West. Tony was always regarded as the vanguard and renaissance man of the group we grew up in, and I was always the follower and did what he said. I read the book like it was liquid morphine flowing into my veins. I couldn't stop and devoured it in short order. By the time I finished the book I knew that I had to follow in this mysterious and magical monk's footsteps—I knew I had to become a monk and study meditation to its end.

Shortly after the week of rain ended, Tony realized he was also unhappy and decided to leave the company and move back to the small town we grew up in called Homewood. I had become quite the salesman and brushman for our little business, and he knew I'd be fine without him.

During the next month of running the business solo, I hired a worker to man the driveway jobs while I managed accounts and got new clients. However, my mind was focused on my exit and escape to the jungle. I was committed to finding a place where I could live as a homeless wandering monk and attain self-mastery... but where could I do that? Oddly enough my eldest sister Rose had done something similar when she was my age. I consulted with her and sought guidance. Kauai, Hawaii was her answer. She had lived on Kauai for about a year and learned how to survive in the wild gathering coconuts, finding wild bananas, and living out of a tent. She was resourceful and always made the right connections when in need. She decided to train me for a month and then return home.

If nothing is your fault then you are never going to be in control or have power over any situation.

It's easy to blame others and never be at fault. Reactive attitudes allow everyone and everything to be the source of all that is wrong. You'll never be responsible for a mistake so long as you can assign blame to someone else. "It's their fault, they aren't close to the operation and cannot see what we see down in the trenches," is a common excuse made by people who don't see their bosses frequently. Reactive attitudes will always assign blame to the thing "out there." They have to in order to be safe. What's the alternative? Be proactive.

Being proactive means taking initiative, anticipating the needs of others and taking the blame for your own and others' mistakes. How else can a solution become possible? Someone has to be proactive, unemotional and detached enough so that progress and moving forward is possible. If proactivity doesn't happen, then you have a team of unproductive blamers that will seek to point the finger at all costs. This type of reactive mindset will never have the courage to be at fault, and forever demand that someone or something else must have gone wrong for the situation to end up where it did. The responsibility for a solution now remains out of sight for the team, and is in a field of unknown and unexplored possibilities as the wrongdoer is out there, somewhere. To be untouched by the responsibility of leadership is a tactic sought out by a certain age group that humans classify as children.

A deposit in terms of banking is similar to the deposits made with the people we interact with every day. In an ideal situation we make a deposit into the emotional bank account of another person. A withdrawal is also similar, you either take out of the bank account and lose money, or you withdraw from someone's emotional account and lose respect.

The goal in being proactive is to simply make more deposits than withdrawals with people and relationships. An example of a deposit would be a compliment, maybe just a smile, or a suggestion for your boss on a project. You get the idea, it's an action that benefits the relationship. A withdrawal could be having an attitude, being jealous at someone for getting the promotion, or not even being sensitive enough to sense someone else's needs. We want to avoid withdrawals and make deposits.

There is a fundamental rule that goes with deposits and withdrawals. The more you are around someone on a daily basis the more deposits you need to make in the emotional bank account. The less you're around someone the more you can rely on older deposits. For example: A family member versus an old friend you haven't seen in ten years—with the old friend you can rely on previous deposits. You have to, right? However, people that you live or work with on a daily basis need constant deposits. This is one of the ways we become proactive. We take charge of our relationships by making deposits with people.

One of the ways you can check if you're doing this is to listen to your language. Listen to the way you communicate with loved ones and coworkers. Are you verbally reassuring people when you speak? Giving them psychological air to breathe? Most of the time people just want to be reassured that you are listening to them. Real listening is not listening with the intent to speak but just listening. They want to know that they are valued, and that their ideas matter to you. Try this today with the people you talk to at home and at work. Are you accidentally verbally abusing people? Speaking out of turn? Not giving someone room to be themselves? Make constant deposits into the emotional bank account of others and you will gain their respect and admiration. Then you can actually work as a team using synergy.

* * *

One by one I let my family know my plans with a phone call or personal visit. My mother knew that I would eventually do something like this, she had seen it in her two daughters before me and did the same thing herself when she was younger. You could call it "soul searching," but in my mind I was renouncing or giving up all that I had and knew for a grand lifelong mission. I was ready to die in the jungle.

My middle sister, Karen, was also not surprised as she had her time of travel and soul searching years before me in Spain. The only member of the family that couldn't quite understand was my father, Maurice. In his eyes I was going to be a beach bum so he made a deal with me.

"I'll buy your ticket to Hawaii if you come with me to New Orleans and help clean up the mess down there." The proposition was simple enough, I agreed and we went.

I will quote Wikipedia to catch you up to speed, "Hurricane Katrina was an extremely destructive and deadly Category 5 hurricane that made landfall on Florida and Louisiana in August 2005, causing catastrophic damage; particularly in the city of New Orleans and the surrounding areas."

My father's deal was made some time in 2006, so it had been several months since the hurricane had touched land. However, damage to the area was so extensive that cleanup and restoration was needed long after Katrina left. Maurice, a few of his friends, and I drove down from Chicago and stayed near the Ninth Ward for seven days. We had the opportunity to work with Acorn, a non-profit organization whose mission was to gut the rotting drywall out of homes in order to save them. The issue, from my understanding, was that if a resident's home had not been gutted from the damage then it would be knocked down. That's as much as I knew and never cared to explore more details, besides I was focused on my adventure that would happen just days later. However, the experience itself was humbling. Witnessing the destruction and the impact it had on people impressed my mind with the power of nature and the inherent weakness man has over her. In just a few moments the entire life of a family can be wiped away, not to mention the larger picture of thousands of people becoming displaced in just a few mere moments.

The work was difficult but rewarding. Every house we worked in was another foundation that could remain standing, so we were trying to beat the clock and work quickly enough to hit multiple homes in a day. We had a volunteer crew of about 10 to 12 people, and we were split up into rooms. I was always with my father and we would remove the rotted drywall and put it into large debris bins to be taken outside, which were then emptied into a large dump truck. We wore suits and face masks to protect ourselves from contamination and disease. (Just prior to us entering a house, it could have been filled with the bodies of people that had stayed, attempting to ride out the coming onslaught of the hurricane.)

I'll never forget the experience and how it made me feel while doing the work. And being there with my father made it one of the few, selfless, service opportunities I ever had with him. The group we were a part of was also honored at a Southern Baptist-style church where the singing was beautiful and touching, and solidarity could be felt from miles away.

I love those types of church gatherings because people don't just read from a book and send you on your way. What they do is attempt to grab whatever God there is from the heavens and pull on that spirit until it sinks down into them. The fun and soul-nourishing worship of those people remain in my heart. The profound thing is, these were the people whose homes we'd been in; whose walls we tore down in order to restore them and they knew it. They thanked us the only way they could, by bringing the joy and love of their divinity down and into our own body. And these people did it with as much fervor and devotion as others with quadruple the amount of possessions and blessings in life. Here they were, devastated and ecstatic. At the same time, they knew full well that the same God who allowed everything to be washed away, could and would just as easily bring abundance back into their lives. That's a mystery that we don't need to understand but we do need to keep and hold onto for as long as we can. It's that very mystery that has kept man going forward into the dark and unknown future since our feet first walked the Earth. It is the potential promise of all unexplored territory that makes the devastation and sorrow of life worth living.

Section 2: Leadership

The end of blaming others is the beginning of leading your own life.

Imagine taking the blame and claiming your own destiny in a world of responsibility. Oddly enough, it will be the most freeing exercise you can put yourself through. Try it. Take the blame and own up to it all. Become a leader if you aren't already one; become a better leader if you already manage a team. Embrace adulthood, stop blaming others, and realize that everything is your fault and we can change anything that is our fault.

When the little things in life become your fault they will also become your responsibility. And I'm talking about starting with micro-decisions that begin in the home and expand throughout your life, beyond the walls of your sanctuary. Take on as much as you can as something you could have done better and faster; or see things as something you could have avoided or planned better. Watch out for the little moments that attack others— even if it is seemingly small and harmless. In the end, whatever happens to you and loved ones could have been a part of your purview instead of an afterthought.

Importantly, remember the golden caveat with taking on this much ownership: Just because anomaly occurs and things go wrong, or people get hurt, doesn't mean you hurt someone or could have saved them. The philosophy of everything being your fault means you are now allowed to fix anything that goes wrong so long as you take responsibility in the moments after it happens.

* * *

Throughout the months of my transition away from the mainland, I'd spent some time resolving my life so I could leave without leaving a trace. I was working the day-to-day business operations with the help of an employee, and now that I was back from New Orleans I had to inform him that I was going away and this chapter in my life was over. All the while, my good friend and drug dealing compadre Sam had been detained for a wrongful charge of weapons trafficking. He didn't have any weapons but when you find as much drugs in someone's apartment as they did in his it doesn't really matter what charge they have, you lose. Sam's intent to distribute was a felony and it was going to make it awfully hard for him to get anywhere in life. I decided he would be the perfect candidate to lead the business and I passed all my accounts on to him. I even offered the truck but he had procured his own in no time at all.

We started from the top of the list and worked our way down, shaking hands and making pleasantries with all my clients, informing everyone that this was the new man to talk to. Sam took the initiative he was known for and got his own accounts early on. He quickly moved from driveways and parking lots to entire apartment complexes and the biggest restaurants in town. Sam was set, and the company Tony and I started was in the best hands we could have ever hoped for.

My sister and I were set to fly in early November if my memory is correct. We needed jackets in Chicago as the weather was changing from autumn to brisk and sharp cold. When we got our plane tickets from my father it was official, and I started to inform friends closest to me that I was indeed leaving the mainland and possibly never coming back. I was treated to drinks, lunches, and dinners before the final day. Even fathers, mothers, and brothers of friends came around to say their goodbyes and wish me a safe journey. People had gathered for a going away party at my good friend Adam's house. Tony and I played guitar, the curious inquired and tried to explore my entire journey all in one night. It was an intimate experience for all really. My own mission had forced everyone around me to reflect on their own.

I'll never forget the truly genuine remarks and reflections close friends had passed down to me. Adam's brother confided in me that it was rare to find such purpose so early on in life and he wished me all the best. Another good friend I grew up with mentioned that even though he was going off to be a starting major league baseball player—and I going off to the jungle penniless and naked (don't worry I had clothes)—that somehow he was getting the short end of the stick. Oddly enough, removing myself from the circle of people that helped raise me was liberating. I felt like a caged bird flying for the first time. I had known hardship and struggle but I was opening myself to the possibility of love—something truly foreign to me up until this point.

The journey of all people begins with discomfort, failure, and the unknown. It is only when we embrace these challenges that we finally become what we were meant to be.

Every day you are going to wake up, walk outside, and enter a moral and ethical bowl of soup. The world is filled with a variety of mental states, different past experiences and a myriad of perspectives of right and wrong. There is not going to be a perfect situation or example to guide you along. Your character will be tested; your opinions and feelings will be challenged by others; and someone at some time is going to attempt to change your perspective so that you adopt theirs. Welcome, now let me present mine.

Life is supposed to present challenges and it does so using our interactions with other people. The challenge is for our benefit and will eventually shape or break us. Getting comfortable with life's hard-hitting nature and even holding out your chin in embracement of it all is the end result of complete maturity and growth. Eventually, we get good at taking shit from others.

In a small book of lectures titled *The Stuff of Manhood*, author Robert Speer outlines his philosophy of excellence to a 1917 American audience. His work pertains to the nature of virtue and how the ethics of a nation should exist within the individual, specifically the aspects related to a militaristic ideal of discipline. Speer suggests that the strict ideals of proper military should reflect personal beliefs, morals, attitudes, and actions. In the book's first lecture titled "Discipline and Austerity," whether we agree on our nation's values or not, Speer recommends the individual inherit the principles of a military's foundation of self-discipline, obedience to our higher nature, and enjoying hardships.

... whatever our views may be on this familiar question, whether we regard military service as ethically helpful in its influence or as morally injurious, we cannot differ as to the need in our national character of those qualities of self-control, of quick and unquestioning obedience to duty, of joyful contempt of hardship, and of zest in difficult and arduous undertakings which, rightly or wrongly, we consider soldierly... To put these primary and elemental needs as sharply as possible, let us call them discipline and austerity. Our American character needs more of both.

Speer is not wrong about what man ought to bring himself to and neither does man fall short permanently. Life is cyclical in nature and people are always returning back to themselves in an act of defiance and hope that they can be better, live better, and act in harmony with their spirit. The genius in Speer's words will never be cliché because someone will always be coming up out of the grind of life having fallen and gotten lost. Another person will always be succeeding in life, ready to take on new challenges as they get back on track from an otherwise stale perspective. Both situations require constant effort. On the one hand, the fallen spirit must yearn to rise up; and on the other, the triumphant must continuously remind themselves of their roles and goals in life with service to others finally becoming the main goal.

Discipline in military training is the example in Speer's lecture as it is a familiar reference point that anyone can understand. When we are confused about where to go, we can always refer back to a soldier's perspective and being part of a group with common beliefs. The tribe mentality syncs well with redefining a person's lot in life because humans are inherently attracted to the qualities and character of solid, concrete, and personal perfecting systems. Man will naturally hold the seed of mastery within, but whether it grows and blooms into a fully formed structure of dynamic effectiveness is the cause for reflection.

The Easy Way or the Hard Way

The whole point of discipline and austerity is to become unshakable. Why do we want to become unshakable? Because life, while sometimes seeming to grant us our every wish, is not that easy when we start to reach beyond what we are normally capable of. Once we endeavor to pass the comfort of our surroundings and enter into unexplored land we inevitably run into competition, jealousy, backbiting, ladder-climbing, cut-throat politics, and consumerism. Life never holds simplicity so long as we are constantly seeking that which is going to make us different and offer change.

Speer's book of lectures doesn't beg us to tie our shoes and tuck in our shirts in hopes that we understand what he's talking about; it says that one day we won't actually have a choice. Boy and girl either become man and woman, or become lost, discontent, unhappy and dissatisfied with the world.

> For a man to love himself so much that he never thinks of his neighbors, to blind his eyes so completely to consequences that he can live for the passing moment,—this is a very easy philosophy, and the man or the woman who is able to practice it will seem, for a while, to live in the sunshine, a fine butterfly, smooth-going life. All this is easier than to say, not, What is my impulse? but, What ought I? not, What do I like? but, What is best for all the world? not, What is the easy way? but, What is the hard way over which the feet go that carry the burdens of mankind, that bear the load of the world? But, though it is the easy way for a while, there comes a time when it is no longer the easy way.

Your mind is going to seek the easier way like water seeks the path of least resistance. The mind's job is to keep you safe and sound but inadvertently weakens your willpower. While the mind is allowed to take over and cloak its master in a special blanket of safety, the real spirit on the inside loses its identity.

Everything is alright, we are all safe and no one is struggling or getting tired, the mind will say. As soon as a challenge comes along, we will crumble. It could be at work when your boss asks you to push on a new front and expand the department, or in traffic when someone tails you and all you want to do is slam on the breaks and force them into a collision—as if that helps. From small to large, mundane to extreme, life tests our capacity for stress and finds a way to see how much pressure we can hold before cracking. Those who wish to have smooth sailing instead of a bumpy road can have their mediocrity. But, as Speer suggests, real joy lay deep within the caverns of self-mastery.

> There comes a time when, having always indulged ourselves, we can't break the habit; when, never having taken our lives in our hands and reined them to the great ministries of mankind, we discover that we cannot. We find that we obey our caprices; follow any impulse; cannot stick to any task; do not know a principle when we see it; have no iron or steel anywhere in our character; are the riffraff of the world that the worthy men and women have to bear along as they go.

If you have ever had the opportunity to understand vice then you know exactly why we seek virtue—contentment. To abide in your own greatness is something to behold. Man truly is an island of self-sufficiency and worth, once he reaches the shores of his own virtues. We can find these people in society or in stories of great heroes or those who acted bravely when called upon. That great soul is defined by Speer,

> The men and women who will not run away from any task, who stand steadfast in truth, upon whose every word we

can rest our whole soul, grew out of a certain discipline and education. And it is this that gives freedom. There is no freedom outside of character. Liberty, as Montesquieu says, is not freedom to do just as we please. Liberty is the ability to do as we ought. And the freedom that we need is not the freedom of caprice and whim and listening to our impulses. It is the freedom that enables our eyes clearly to see what right is, and then empowers us to do it.

Many of the issues surrounding young developing minds—short attention span, social conditioning, insecurities—can be found to take root by being ensconced inside social media. Social media, or any form of instant communication, can be a type of drug. Instagram might not look like your typical narcotic, but when you dissect what happens in the brain when unending scrolling takes place, your brain lights up with dopamine and you get excited, one scroll after another. The labyrinth of notifications, instant change and novelty is conveniently right in your hand but acts as a double-edged sword. Learn to strategize and make plans to balance social media with real face-to-face contact and the reading of actual books.

The light of a starry night sky is better and more healing than anything a digital picture can offer. How can you even have a conversation on Reddit without constant refreshing of the page, god that is depressing isn't it? If you never train yourself to absorb the beauty of nature, and its innate abundance and silence, then all of your energy will be pulled out as you seek another form of excitement and novelty. The Internet alone is truly a grand phenomenon that when taken to excess is a sure cause for illness. When used with discipline, though, these things can be a game-changer in regards to work and social systems. But if you don't have any inner capacity for strength or restriction, these things will drag you along in their endless variety.

And we must learn in this school (of life) the things we value and desire most—purity and delicacy and refinement of character, for they cannot be acquired elsewhere. So much social standing nowadays is uttered in terms of self-assertion and indulgence and the ability to have any whim or caprice gratified. This sort of self-assertion, this caprice, is regarded by many of us as the highest mark of social authority, whereas we know it is precisely the opposite, that it is self-restraint and self-control and self-surrender that mark the finest lives.

The Need to Fight

Some of us grow up in angry homes and hostile communities. Either kids are fighting at school; parents are fighting in the home; or we witness high emotions and anger in politics and world events. People are base, crass, rude, and ineloquent creatures that think it is okay to lose one's cool and fight back against the world's injustice with more anger, violence, and injustice. They are wrong and they look ridiculous.

Developmentally, it is natural for children to retaliate or act out. Little boys and girls name-call and use silly one-liners to attack their schoolmates. However, adults are supposed to grow out of these habits. Our brains finish developing and we can learn to make our minds into a respectable place where discussion and conversation can happen in a healthy way. Getting back to maturity means we have to get a little more intellectually astute and a little less brute.

Advice for Men (Yang)

By default, men are more aggressive, more protective, more demanding and certainly the male sex is physically stronger and prone to defending that reputation. There's nothing wrong with learning how to defend oneself—many great men were also boxers—but we have to know when and where to throw punches and be pugilistic.

Getting angry, or even getting overly emotional, shows that you are prone to letting your defenses down and letting immediate gratification take over. We only resort to that because we do not yet know what it feels like to outwit someone or be the bigger man and let something go. The bigger man wins in the long run, the angry fool remains the same. If you are to exude leadership then you have to be the kind of soul that knows right from wrong and does not answer to any immoral decision. This goes into our private life as well. If you are willing to reach towards pleasure over wisdom when alone, you are sure to show weakness in public.

For Women (Yin)

Are you able to spend more time around children, hold them and transfer a loving energy that simply cannot be transferred through a man or words? Harnessing the feminine energy of creation is not easy, and it will cause much disruption in your life if you haven't begun educating yourself about your own power—use it for good.

Women should try their hand at a creative art like music, singing, drawing, writing, acting, dancing, and public speaking. I know women want to take on the world, and any woman with the will should, but know that staying close to family—the tribe— will ultimately give you the greatest support in your endeavors. Staying close to mom and siblings, keeping the family together (especially eldest sisters), keeping open lines of communication with friends and learning elegance will balance out your home, your life, your mind and spirit. And yes, your Yang, your balance in the home depends on someone that can help absorb the chaos from which divine feminine energy creates, not help create more chaos. The concept of Yin and Yang don't necessarily refer to a man or a woman, but to those energies that are dominant in the individual. A gay or lesbian couple can still use the ancient reference of Yin and Yang if they observe what energies are predominant inside themselves and seek to balance them.

> Once more. Whose judgment is of any value? What does passion bid me do? What is my whim or caprice for tonight? No men will ever come to you and me if we have not been trained in the school of moral discrimination, if we have not looked on ethical principle and duty in deciding the question whether each thing is really right for us and for the whole world. If we are to be men and women to whom people will come for comfort and strength and guidance, to whom our own children can come with assurance that they will get the truth, we must be men and women who now place ourselves beneath the firm discipline of God (our higher nature).

This idea of taking on burden for the purpose of getting stronger is so profound it can't be left out. By living too easily we actually stunt our growth and delay its progress. Speer, a Christian, will ask to "carry your own cross," but followers of any faith can just replace the word cross for burden and you have a foundation in which to live. If you don't have a burden, or cross or any trouble—start to take on service for others and selflessly help and mentor. Take their cross or their karma or their trouble and make it your own. Make your life harder.

> No strong man was ever made against no resistance. We develop no physical power by putting forth no physical effort. All the strength of life we have we get by pushing against opposition. We acquire power as we draw it out of deep experience and effort. Those of us who were not born with a cross must find one, those whose lives have been smooth are to deliberately find ways of roughening them, so that we may know a life of power and fellowship and can go out to real work, and be prepared for that greater life and greater service which await us elsewhere than here.

* * *

I will never forget the moment I unzipped our tent door to see a new world appear before me. The rocks of a small beach held us for the night, giving us the structure we needed to pitch a tent and feel secure. I smelled the Hawaiian air and knew I was home. The events that took place those first few weeks of my new life freed me from the shackles of normalcy and left me without ties to anyone, anything, or anyplace. Waking up early on the remote beaches surrounded by nothing except the occasional seal digesting its meal on shore, hours of chanting OM and meditating, going over the details of surviving the years with nothing—that homeless period of my life was absolutely blissful. The power behind my disciplines, the freedom from worldly attachment, it was all perfect and to this day I can't believe it unfolded the way it did. I was free and I knew I had made the right choice.

Kauai's Hindu Monastery was always in the back of my mind having been shown the website before leaving the mainland, but it was far, far back in there as a "maybe." *Surely they wouldn't take in some homeless wanderer*, I thought, as the chances diminished the longer I thought about it. The weeks went by quickly but I was confident that I could get by without my sister. After one month of daily meditation and chanting for hours on end, I knew I still needed a teacher—a guide who had achieved what I was trying to achieve. It wasn't survival that I was worried about; it was the fact that I didn't know my own mind or the techniques to master it.

My time with Rose went quickly. We would rise, bathe in the ocean, and enjoy the day. Sometimes she would take me to certain spots in town to increase my navigation skills and mental map of the island, other times we stayed on the beach all day writing, chanting, and talking about life. My goal was never a mystery to Rose. That's something I had never quite realized (until now as I write this section of the book). She was a free spirit and knew herself. She knew what she wanted in life, what made her happy and how to get it. I had never really known her well as she was older and she moved out when I was still young. She left in order to find herself, travel the world, and meet other people, cultures and traditions. We took this time to talk about where I thought meditation could take me and how I might get there. She never doubted me, she loved and cared for me—her little brother.

We traveled every third day so we didn't make ourselves known. Never staying in one place too long to attract any attention. On travel day we packed up and walked, sometimes needing the machete she carried to clear the way. I carried an axe so I could crack coconuts and drink the water. Rose showed me how to snag a vine of coconuts growing from tall trees with the axe and some rope. I'd tie the axe to the rope, fling it up high in the air at the string of coconuts and hope it wrapped around or hooked the top of the bunch. Then, I'd either pull on the rope and try to bring down the bunch or, if there was slack, I'd use the weight of the axe to come down to Rose so we both could pull. We could gather about four coconuts and attach them to my pack for travel. Other times we would snag wild bananas off the highway and carry them to our next camp. Once settled and unpacked we never foraged, that was only during travel. The trick was to land, settle and not venture too far from the area. That way no one could follow us in and give us any trouble.

The time came for my sister to start thinking about her flight home and getting back to her life in society. She asked that I give the monastery a call so she would know I at least tried to improve my living situation. (It's possible my sister didn't completely trust my skills in the wild.) So I called the monastery and mentioned I was a seeker in need of training in the art of meditation, specifically Raja yoga. The monk on the phone said, "When are you planning on visiting the island?" After finding out I had already arrived and was not far from the monastery, he said I should come for a tour and we would talk afterwards.

Meanwhile, I noticed we had slowly moved closer to people and civilization. Instead of our usual remote sandy beach spots, we had ventured into a beach park called Salt Pond for the last week of her stay. Salt Pond has an actual salt collection area where the locals collect salt. The sunrise and sunsets are stunning at this little beach park. The shore is shaped like a bay, letting the water collect around a giant circle, protecting swimmers from Kauai's rough undercurrents.

Rose was mentally done with the training, getting herself ready to enter civilization yet again, letting go of the jungle-hermit life. She spent more time meeting people and bringing me out with her new friends. The Salt Pond Crew was what they called themselves. They were a group of locals who gathered at the beach park after work to drink a few beers, play the ukulele, and make fun of each other. They took a liking to Rose and I and eventually invited us over to share a meal. We spent the next few days cruising around the island in their convoy, going to all the beautiful unseen spots tourists know nothing about—nor having the vehicles to get them there. We were having a blast and they loved my story and what I wanted to do. "You're gonna live like a monk or something and meditate all day?" was the normal local question. "Ya, something like that," is as simple of an answer as I could respond with. "Shoots, braddah," was an easy way to end a conversation in pure Hawaiian style, not too complex or overthought.

This was around Thanksgiving, 2006, and so some wonderful locals invited us to their home for the holiday. We ate and talked about our lives and what we wanted to do with ourselves. My path was well received by everyone we met and it was clear that an innate sense of spirituality existed among the Kauai'an population. Many gave me their blessings for a long and rich life whether in a monastery or jungle, and everyone had good things to say about the "monks on the hill," and they were sure that they would let me in. It seemed I was the only skeptical one of the group.

Ultimate peace does not come from living in the jungle but from within yourself.

People will travel and seek far outside themselves for that one thing that brings ultimate peace and long-lasting happiness; yet, all the while their issues and problems are right underneath their feet. We cannot simply remove ourselves from our challenges. Insecurities, addictions, fears, regrets and sorrow all originate from within ourselves. Our mind is the very thing that needs updating and refreshing, not the location of where our body is on a map. Wherever we travel to we bring ourselves with, and if we aren't comfortable in New York City then we won't find lasting peace in Jamaica sipping cocktails on the beach and reading our favorite book. NYC can be hectic and chaotic, and the hustle and bustle of the city could cause stress that eventually ruins your mental equanimity—but the problem is not with NYC, it's with you. Eventually our past trauma and burdens—and even our lack of structure and discipline—come out from deep inside the mind to remind us who we really are, what we're made of and how much we can endure.

"But that's exactly what you did," you may say. And it's true, I left society in order to focus on myself, but soon enough in the story you will see how all of my immaturities came out once the monks put me to work. Just because I took vows and became a monk didn't mean my mind had changed in the slightest. The maturation process took years and years of work. I did not become brand new by just reading out a few vows on a piece of paper and wearing robes.

I'm frequently asked by disillusioned young men if they should do what I did and join a monastery. Of course, that's the way I felt at the age of 19 and indeed I dropped everything, moved to a monastery in the jungle, and lived a 12 year life of discipline inside an institution that specialized in self-mastery and individual enlightenment.

Did that solve all my problems? No, in fact the problems I had with the world followed me to the jungle and haunted me. Later I realized that I was in fact the problem, and I needed a community to help me find discipline and structure. I used that perspective to solve myself, and thus falling in love with the twofold path of a healthy world: moderation and balance. I now have healthy desires based on moderation, and I can find balance in the spiritual and worldly.

Did the monastery help? Yes, but is it the only way? No. There are lots of communities focused on self-discipline, balance, moderation, psychology, meditation, and well-being.

Would I do it again? Yes, I would. Why? I'm an all or nothing kind of soul. I'm either all in or nothing at all, and that's what balances me. After all, balance and moderation are self-defined. The military-like discipline, schedule, and structure—and the pains of struggling through psychological breakdowns—are the things I secretly long for. I'm most happy when life is hard, I'm near dead, and the only way to survive is by my own sheer determination, and against all odds. Are you me? If you are, then get out of the world and live in a community that harbors discipline, find structure, ritual, and routine that will help you discover yourself. But, be careful, because you will end up realizing what I did. The monastery you seek is inside your mind.

* * *

Tour day at the monastery came and a friend named Joe, who was part of the Salt Pond Crew, gave me a ride in his little white pickup truck. I offered him to join but he casually said no thanks, "It's your thing." I climbed out of the little truck and stood in line at the entrance and waited for 9am. As I stood there the person in front of me quietly asked, "Are you supposed to be in front?" I was silent and puzzled for a moment and then chuckled while saying, "I think we are all in this together!" My guess is that the woman asked because of my outfit. The one thing my father gave me before I left for the island was a long beautiful silk gown called a *kurta* that he was gifted from an Indian man at his work. The long silk kurta was way too big for me and went from my neck down to my feet. I think it had an elegance to it that some found regal.

There was something special about the monastery, something incredibly sacred was going on and you could feel it when you walked onto the property just beyond the gates. I knew very quickly into the tour that this would be the perfect place for me to train and become a master of meditation.

After the tour I waited just outside the temple on the sidewalk for the monk who wanted to speak about training. The tour-guiding monk, Satyanatha, noticed I was idle and kindly asked if I needed something. I mentioned I was there to see someone about monastic training and, like magic, the monk I was there to see arrived and introduced himself. Satyanatha gave a sweet chuckle and said, "Yes, that's how things happen around here!" The tall and medium build bearded monk and I exchanged pleasantries and we both gazed at each other for a moment. Soon into the discussion I discovered that I had to leave. "You can't stay here for training," this soft-toned monk said in a way that wasn't offensive at all. "There is paperwork and, well, you can't just jump into this."

"Okay," I said hiding my frustration, "it's either here or back to the woods then. So, no big deal."

"What about your family? What is your plan?"

"I left the world in order to master meditation and that's what I'm going to do," I said with the conviction of a child not wanting to nap. I've never done anything half-hearted and I wasn't going to let this change my dedication to my path but I hadn't yet learned how to be graceful in expressing myself and explaining my passions. Neither of us wasted any time. The monk wished me well and I turned around heading back to camp.

Joe was napping in the parking lot as I came up to the car. He asked how it went and I updated him on my revoked status with the monks. Joe leaned in close to me and said with his sweet chubby grin, "It's their loss." After arriving back at camp I used my phone for the second time since arriving on Kauai and did what any lost and confused teenager would do: I called my mom.

"They won't take me in for training. I got denied, Ma." To my surprise my mother gave me one of the most profound and lasting pieces of advice I've ever received, "They're testing you, my dear. Go back every day." She continued after I fell silent, "Find work to do, ask questions, be present and interested in the mission, not just what you want. Go back to the temple every day and don't take no for an answer."

Along my journey I have had so many teachers, mentors and guides that helped land me where I am today—but no teacher is quite like Mom. We all have them somewhere, moms are every human's first teacher but many don't see them like that. In order for us to successfully embrace the chaotic and unexplored world we must leave her side, and maybe it is then that we realize what we were being shielded from. It's mom's job to protect and even conceal to make sure we don't see the unknown and terrible world too soon. The world of burden, challenge and hardship is then revealed to us in small portions (some get it in large portions all up front) as we venture out and away from the nest. If we don't get matured into chaos slowly, and the very support system that was supposed to shield us from doom actually creates our suffering, then all hell breaks loose as we lack the training, guidance and foundation from that which was to be solid: mom. In the end we have to thank our parents for their attempt at their job, and everyone has a different approach. A lot of my work now is to try and undo the mistakes that parents have made while raising their children. "Forgive them for they know not what they do..." comes to mind when I think of parents. Some get it right, some don't, and some have a mixture of right and wrong. Since extended families aren't all that common anymore and tribes are spreading out in a global world, parents are left to decide what to do without the help of wisdom from older generations. Adults in today's world are doing the best with what they have, and sometimes that isn't all that much. But surely we must admit that we were brought into a world of chaos all the while trying to make order of everything, and one of the best tools we could have ever asked for is a mom, whether good, bad or somewhere in between—we all learned something from her, and that's better than nothing.

A leader never succeeds alone, there's always someone or something they can thank for their success.

People have always asked me how to handle narcissists as if they are a poison of society needing to be cleansed from our view. The definition of a narcissist is someone with an inflated sense of self-worth, lack of empathy for others and an excessive need for admiration. Basically every leader, entrepreneur, inventor, or creator falls into the category of narcissist, and the negative context and rising popularity of the word itself has been a red flag and call to arms to protect society from these ego-driven maniacs.

Most of us fall into the category of narcissist somewhere along the spectrum. Without some of those qualities I'm not sure what kind of impact you can have in the world. Leaders, organizers, business owners and corporate figureheads need their ego in order to manipulate the physical forces of the world, and without their overinflated sense of worth nothing would get better; nothing would change. Modern life today is a beautiful and fast-paced world, with ease-of-living improving so quickly. We have more time to spend with loved ones, experiencing new things more than any other time period that came before. It truly is a great time to be alive and the ego-driven, narcissistic-like groups and individuals are part of the success.

But where do we draw the line? What qualities can help balance out a strong leader so ego doesn't dominate relationships? A good leader must empower the team around them, remember and give praise to every stepping stone on their path that helped get them where they are today. The best leaders also take the most blame.

* * *

How am I going to get across island every day to the monastery? I thought to myself after getting off the phone with Mom. The challenge was that I was situated in another town far from the monastery and unable to casually walk to and from every day. My sister was a traveler and she was prone to leaving camp and coming back by the end of the day. Meanwhile, I stayed behind to study, reflect, meditate and chant. The next day after my disappointing news she came back to Salt Pond from the library not far from where we were camped with a small pocketbook. On the back of the little book was the founder of the monastery.

"I thought you might like this, I think it's about meditation or something." I heard what my sister said but couldn't take my eyes off the book or the picture of the head monk.

"This is him!" I shouted to my sister. "This is the monk who started it all!" Rose, now packing our bags and camp, finished her thought without understanding the profundity that was now occurring in my world and said, "We're leaving the wild, I got offered to stay with a friend near the airport so I can easily catch my flight in a few days."

"Oh?" I said puzzled. "Why don't I stay here at camp? Besides, I'm not flying anywhere."

She stopped packing in order to look at me in the eyes and said, "Because my friend lives near the monastery and you will be in walking distance and can visit there every day. After I leave you may return to the woods."

You can imagine the blank look on my face as I pondered the sequences that made up my life. How? Was the universe in my favor? Regardless, I didn't have much to pack nor could I answer such deep reflections at the moment. Quickly gathering my life into a small bag and swinging it over my shoulder, I followed Rose to the parking lot to meet her new friend and make my way up the hill.

Leading a team is like leading our own life but with a team we expand the amount of blame that we take.

The greater the responsibility, the greater the opportunity for blame. Great people throughout history have been able to absorb the mistakes of others and I suggest that you do the same. Why is it that the most honorable figures in time have taken the most blame? Somehow in some way there is an ancient trait, story or myth—a kind of shared agreement—among humans, to revere those who can take the most blame and suffering. Look at any religious epic and myth—the figurehead, or the one who is most revered, usually ends up taking the blame for all of mankind.

A common theme among monastic orders is to become disciples of a Great One—a Buddha, a Christ, a Messiah of some kind—and join in on relieving the suffering of the many by attempting to absorb it all for oneself. Isn't that the mark of a saint? There's something about our ancient mythologies, cultures and traditions that reveres human sponges of sacrifice. Not only that, but within these ancient teachings and motives there's an innate sense and teaching that we are born into sorrow—as if it isn't our choice but to experience pain, challenge and hardship. These figures throughout history one-up everyone by seeing the trend of individual suffering, and take it upon themselves for the masses. This sacrifice, this eternal enduring of punishment for the sake of relieving others, is then worshipped by those needing relief. And why not? It's easier if someone takes all the blame, then we just thank and worship them for their sacrifice and call it good. But, what I'm suggesting is that we become the saints of our own individual realities. We take on however much we can and reap the consequences. The alternative is to let someone else do it for you, and we all know how that goes in the long run. It's not only better to take the blame ourselves for the sake of others, but it's offering some form of sacredness into your life by doing something holy, something that most aren't able to do. The result of this kind of proactivity is increasing our circle of influence.

The circle of influence is the amount of people that need us in decision making. The more deposits we make into the emotional bank account of others, the more our circle of influence grows. You think one person can be affected? Try thinking about 10 or 20. What if 100 people looked up to you for guidance. Extending your circle of influence to more and more people makes you vulnerable because people will try to take advantage of that. Before opening yourself up, you have to learn about the win-win and win-lose. Be strong about your time, don't be the "nice guy" if you're the one losing out of the deal, always go for the win-win.

Being proactive or being effective can happen instantly if you know how to take blame effectively. We have to think about the other person's next move and give them help before they ask. The key principle is we sense the needs of the individual. By doing so you become a listener and open your circle of influence so large that people will begin to need your input on matters that are important to them. The details are complex but that's the immediate practice. Take the blame and responsibility by sensing the needs of other people. Sometimes all we have to do is be open to someone's concern and give them psychological air. This means we are letting someone breathe around us and we don't constrict them. We are open to their thoughts and feelings without judging, without manipulating. An example of this is empathy, or feeling the way the other person does without agreeing or disagreeing.

The opposite end of the spectrum is the circle of concern. This means we have taken too many withdrawals from the emotional bank account with people. We are on thin ice with these people and have created distance. We have to watch everything we say and everything we do. One wrong move and an argument or disagreement occurs. Obviously we don't want this. In this situation, we have to seriously consider making deposits in a planned way. To mend this broken relationship you would have to seek the person out and start aiding their daily life somehow. Ideally, we never get into this situation. We avoid it by taking responsibility for as much as we can thus making the circle of influence larger and larger; the natural consequence being that the circle of concern gets smaller and smaller.

* * *

Waiting for us in the Salt Pond parking lot was Rose's new friend, Chandra, and her two kids. We made the move to Chandra's place up the hill, in a town called Kapaa and, sure enough, it was a 10-minute bike ride away from the monastery. Chandra was a teacher who lived with her two little adorable twin girls. We became good friends rather quickly and soon I was borrowing Chandra's van to take the kids for ice cream in the evenings and riding her bike wherever I wanted to go.

[I ended up running into Chandra years later at the local Home Depot with another monk. She recognized me immediately and was happy to see that I was accomplishing my goals as a monk. Chandra had also changed her life shortly after our stay with her, and she and her daughters reported that she was finally living the life she wanted.]

My early morning routine stayed the same. I woke up before the sun rose, and did my meditation and chanting on the second floor deck of the house long before the roosters took over the countryside. One could see rolling pasture hills as well as palm and citrus trees spread out along the fields. As the sun slowly made its way over the ground you could see each dew drop on the grass blades. (For most of the year the weather on Kauai is warm enough to enjoy those dark hours, but after getting acclimated to the seasons of Kauai I noticed the winters having more effect on me.) I would then borrow Chandra's bike and ride up the quiet farm road to the temple. The monastery gates opened at 9am and sure enough I was early everyday, excited but also trepidatious. I would lock the bike up to a tree in the parking lot and change into my long silk kurta gown and white pants before stepping onto the holy ground.

For the first few days I would grab one of the books provided in the temple and read it outside on a bench, never once staying for the main ceremony that happened every morning at 9:05am. The hour-long ceremony would end with the tintinnabulation of what sounded like a thousand bells and I'd return the book and sit down to meditate until it was time to leave at noon.

After the rush of devotees, it became a blissful quiet place. The temple roof was made with large redwood beams in traditional Japanese carpentry. Beams intersected with such precision one could not tell where one beam began and another ended. The stone walls were four feet thick and supported the wooden beams in perfect harmony. Large mirrors adorned the sides of the wall like art and gave one a sense of unlimited space. Gold-leafed *Tandava* (dancer) statues stood on redwood beam shelving in front of the mirrors. Incense burned constantly and filled the air with a soul-nourishing smoke.

In the back of my mind, I knew I was pushing against the monk who denied my request for training. Part of me thought I was being disobedient and rude by returning like I did, but I knew what I wanted and my myopic plan left me not knowing what would happen next.

One morning, while I was reading their mystical books outside, a temple caretaker named Shama approached and curtly said, "You can't take the book outside, I'm afraid. Please, come read it inside." Shama was an elderly woman with an elegant English accent—I would later know her very well. She dedicated every day to helping the monks guide people around the public area that comprised the front acreage of the grounds. After becoming an accomplished figure skater, Shama (her name means patience) served her guru for decades and eventually moved to the island, along with several other dedicated disciples, and devoted her life to her guru's mission.

After stepping over the large granite threshold that separated that which was outside and inside, and sitting down on the lavender carpet to continue reading, Shama came by again and insisted I should read later and join the ceremony called Puja, or "worship with flowers." I did as she said and got up to join the worship.

The head priest who performed the daily ceremony saw me join in for the first time and gave me a penetrating look as he passed the sacraments around. Once the worship was over I returned to the floor for my daily meditation. Soon after, a bare-chested monk sat down right next to me. He asked who I was and what I was doing (at this point that question was asked so much I had my script ready). I told him I left the world to master meditation and I would stop at nothing to do it. The monk was tall and elegantly thin with a long white beard, silver hair, and blue piercing eyes. His name was Ceyonswami and he'd been a monk for four decades. "Read this section of the book," he told me squarely, taking the book I had been reading and flipping to the last section with his long fingers and perfect pointy fingernails, "this is what you want to read and meditate on." And then he got up and walked away. "My first mission!" I thought excitedly. I returned in the mornings then with purpose and direction.

All permanent change and transformation takes work and diligence. Just begin by taking the blame.

Nothing good and lasting is easy and it takes work to make strides of lasting success—it's hard work that seems impossible. Changing ourselves is possibly the hardest task we can ever embark upon, but it is certainly the most noble endeavor we have to accomplish while here on Earth. It all begins with discontentment—not being happy or satisfied—with our current situation, and it evolves into a vision of where we see ourselves as a new person. Begin by accepting where you are because you did it—you got yourself into this mess and you can get yourself out. That should be a relief!

Take for instance the reason why we feel sorrow or burden in the first place: we lack control over a person or situation. The moment we realize that someone else is making the decisions, we have put us on edge as we go down the rabbit hole of fantasy: we imagine what could go wrong; how much of an imbecile the current leader is; all of our insecurities leave us ready to be taken advantage of by someone else. We're powerless... but there's hope!

Taking responsibility and blame mean you become your own commander-in-chief, your own boss of your own life. That doesn't mean others are going to be perfect. People may never defer to your will and opinion, or even notice you've become responsible—but it isn't any of your business what someone else thinks, anyway. You need to worry about you, so you take your own blame in whatever way you can. You find your own responsibility eventually, even if that means being more effective with someone higher up than you. Bringing ego into the situation is not always going to help. Sometimes, it's best to actually accept that someone other than you is in charge and is making whatever decisions he/she pleases. Our job, then, is about becoming the best first-rate-second-man there is, reading the situation and becoming effective with whomever is in charge.

How can I be effective with them, is the question you should ask yourself. Not, *How am I going to take over?* That's only going to lead to more sorrow because whomever is in charge got there for a reason, good or not, so you need to now accept that and take over your own mind. It's your own mind, your own dominion that emanates self-control and everlasting peace—no matter what's happening on the outside. Don't be quick to rule, take over or overthrow the current regime outside of yourself. Rule the inside of you, your mind, then enjoy the contentment that follows.

* * *

"Someone would like to speak with you…" I was reading in my usual corner, and digesting the material I was told to read several days earlier, when a young monk with calming eyes and a soft voice approached. "… he would like to have tea."

"Yes!" I thought, this was my in. I followed the white-robed monk out of the temple and down a sidewalk that wrapped around a giant mango tree. We went into an office that had several computer workstations and a big desk right in the middle of the floor.

"Well, hello and welcome," said the robed monk sitting at his center space. I will never forget the genuine and sweet air those monks breathed. Their voices and manners were an aid in helping me stay present and focused while my mind could have run through thousands of thoughts and questions. "Thank you," I said demurely, "it's an honor to be here."

The monk who guided me in returned to his desk and my eyes had a chance to follow him and then gaze around the room at the other monks, each one smiling sweetly at me with a warmth that could invite any soul.

"This tea is very good for you," the white-bearded monk mentioned while a young monk poured me a glass, "now, tell me why you are here."

"I want to learn Raja yoga," I told him squarely and with confidence. Raja, or royal, yoga is considered the most ancient form of yoga or union with the divine. A giant smile draped the monk's face and out came an encomium on the greatness of yoga. He allowed me to ask questions and just enjoy the space together. When I finished my tea the monk told me he wanted to have tea with me every day at the same time. I was holding in my joy and said it would be an honor.

I returned to Chandra's and checked back in with my mother; she had gotten me this far so I had to give her an update. She gave her wise counsel yet again, "Now that you are in the door you must ask for work, make their mission your mission. Stop admitting what you want and start to accept what they want."

Over the next few days I returned as requested and sat with the monk to have tea. We talked about many different aspects of monastic life, the path of yoga, meditation, and I finally built up the courage to ask, "How can I stay longer?"

"What do you mean?" the senior monk said with a puzzled gaze.

"I mean, after our tea is over I don't want to leave. I'd like to stay. I want to stay here longer each day and work."

"Oh!" He chuckled at the proposition and then got serious again. "You can go to the forest right outside my office," I was so focused on his direction I couldn't feel my body anymore, "and you'll notice the ground is ridden with massive sticks from the banyan tree. Pick up all of the sticks and leave them in a pile on the edge of the forest. When you finish clearing the floor of the forest, go to the pile and put those sticks on the other side until we tell you to go away."

For several days I picked up sticks from that forest like no one had ever done before. Somehow I knew that everything was working, everything was going according to plan. What plan? No idea, definitely not mine. But I couldn't help feeling a certainty with what I was involved in. I was trusting the process and knew that I was in a sacred place surrounded by sacred people. After several days of doing what I was told, the monk who first said I should go home appeared in the forest. He asked for my picture to give to the head monk, the guru of the monastery. He said thank you and walked away. The next day he appeared again as I cleared the forest floor and said I could stay for the initial six-month training period called Taskforce. I was in.

Everything begins intellectually—in the mind— then manifests into physical reality. Knowing this, the mind should be kept clean and tidy.

We each have a mental blueprint in which to start our next action, whether it is a task, goal, project, or if it is big, small, profound or mundane—they all begin in the same place, the mind. Concepts of the task have already been developed in the mind, we simply act it out in the physical world. In order for things to go according to plan we ought to have good blueprints.

People's minds are cluttered with the debris of past trauma, unresolved situations, and misconceptions about their own being. Most people don't know who they are and possibly never will. This aphorism does two things: first, it asks you to think about where everything comes from, where our reality begins. Second, it asks that we take the creation grounds of our mind and clean them up, thus having the best opportunity at manifesting what we want without any clutter to get in the way.

How do we clean up the mind? A good place to start is spending more time outside getting plenty of fresh air. We need to start putting phones and screens down and placing our bodies outside in the sun where it belongs. When we're ready to begin self-reflecting we will have to face past trauma as well as all of our unresolved mental burdens. That will take time and work but it can be done. Here are some elements to cleaning up the mind indirectly, meaning without going inside it directly, also known as sharpening the saw.

Exercise. Physical movement is the most clear and obvious one. The human body was meant to be more active than it is sedentary. Incorporating fresh air into our lungs, athletic activity, and eating real food. All these habits improve life, and need to be a part of a healthy and balanced one.

Our mental/intellectual upliftment is also self-evident but not always a habit. People tend to graduate from a school system and let this element go by joining the work-force and having a family. Get back to reading, writing, and analytical thinking. Watch less TV. Read a book every month to start. Writing is also very powerful. We need to get back to regular writing since, over time, thoughts build up in our mind and should be written down as a type of clearing for more to come in. As we mature, so do our thoughts. Clearing the mental docket in a journal makes room for future reflections and realizations.

The spiritual value system is the most personal element of the four. The spiritual side of your life needs to be cultivated. This isn't a religious habit; although, it can be. This habit means getting back to who we really are. What makes you, you? Find something that brings real mental peace and contentment. It can be a matter of getting back to nature and just reflecting with friends and family. Camping can be profound if you look at it this way. Cultivate time by yourself and enjoy those moments. Try to not always be around people and doing things. Have a target of mental peace and freedom by scheduling it on the calendar for once a month. Say to yourself: "Once a month I'm going to enjoy silence and be alone. I'm going to reflect on me and what I'm all about. I'm going to stay away from technology and mobile devices during this time." Eventually, we increase this to weekly and then, ultimately, we create daily personal time. This is a private training time that complements the public aspects of life. In fact, this personal time of reflection can change your life in and of itself.

The emotional/social aspects of your life come next, and the two go together because they reflect so strongly on each other. These elements occur naturally if all other elements are adhered to. We automatically shift our paradigm of life and how we relate to that life. As we win private battles, we can become better at winning public ones. We start becoming proactive and adjustments begin to take place. In the end, our character, our attitude towards ourselves, as well as our attitudes towards all people, adjusts to this new way of living.

* * *

I had to wait a few days for the monks to prepare a space for me in the training house just outside the monastery grounds. My sister left during my waiting period and I had a few more chances to get Chandra's kids some ice cream. On the last night before the Taskforce program began, Chandra took me out for one last hurrah at a small local bar with live music. I was too shy to dance but everyone had a good time carousing away like it was their last night of freedom. Only a few in the room knew that it was indeed my last night as a civilian.

As the sun rose the next morning, I was already up practicing my chanting and meditation, possibly with more fervor than ever before. This morning was the day I was going to be admitted into the monastery for basic training that would last six months. The feelings in my stomach, hands, limbs and spirit were vibrant and alive. For the first time in my life I felt like I was beginning a mission; something with purpose and meaning that was just for me, and it was perfect. My timing of arrival could not have been planned better. Just a day before I was set to settle in, Satyanatha, the tour-guiding monk, had finished his training and moved out. He was making the move inside the monastery gates since he was becoming a monk. Each monk received their own ten foot by ten foot stone hut, empty except for a small shrine, bed, and wooden frame.

I was dropped off at the training house located just outside the monastery grounds and greeted by four young students living there. Three of them had been training at the monastery for three months and would be going back home to see their families after three more months. One of the students was almost a monk and would be moving out soon to take vows and get his own hut.

The monks lived in the 100 square foot huts, all concrete, no electricity or running water. They used the stone huts to pray, meditate, sleep, and study.

Leadership roles require willful responsibility.
Willful responsiveness requires effective
communication. First define goals, then roles to
fulfill those goals.

No one can really lead effectively if they don't know they are in charge. After the initial burst of inspiration is over, a leader will generally sink down into the general population, never to take charge in the same situation again, so long as there is no positive reinforcement as backup. In other words, if you don't let someone know they are in charge, or that you want to be in charge, don't expect them or yourself to be effective leaders. Why does this occur? It's human nature to not want to step on toes and be rude, especially in a relationship. How is a man supposed to know he is the natural leader of the family (paterfamilias) when modern ethics and political correctness put masculinity into a blanket paradigm of toxicity? The same relationship challenges exist in the office dynamic. A subordinate with any amount of respect will always try to defer to the boss and not stick out too much, but what if the boss *wants* them to? In both cases it's better to communicate roles so that the agreed-upon goals can be accomplished. This requires effective communication. Let people know they are in charge, and step aside so they can lead.

* * *

My first six months went by blissfully, I was an angel on my best behavior. No arguments, subordinate issues, interpersonal challenges—life in the monastery was exactly what you think it would be: perfect. The monastery had five monk-run departments all referred to with two letters: accounting (PK), temple and kitchen (LK), landscaping and construction (SK), church membership (LK), and publishing (GK).

The students training in their first six months were known as "taskforcers" and they were allowed to make mistakes, call home, use informal speech, talk with mainland friends, watch movies and documentaries. We were fresh, young and nothing serious was expected from us. My job for those six months was to observe the other monks, follow simple directions, and research the life of a monk in order to decide if it was for me.

I spent one month in each of the monastery's departments except for church membership, as that department was only for monks, due to its sensitive nature of people management. I was young, inexperienced and knew nothing, so that kind of work was best left to the mature monks who were ordained priests and counselors.

Our daily schedule was strictly timed but that is what gave us the freedom to do so much within one 24-hour period. I had never given it much thought until I was years into monastic life but our schedule, diet, chain of command, and vows were all based on a militaristic design of structure and simplicity—and I was really good at it. This would have been the first time in my life that I had pure structure and actually followed it. There was nothing complicated about the schedule, just one rule: don't be late. Tardiness was frowned upon and there were consequences for not adhering to the schedule. As young students not yet under vows, there were allowances and exceptions but something was always mentioned in a remark or comment later. It was made clear that for the moment it was okay but, had we been monks, there would be no tolerance for being late.

Roll call started each weekday, which included meeting in the temple in a single-file line in order of rank, at 5:30am. Most of the monks were up by 4am drinking espresso and doing a special set of yoga postures that the monks developed in the early days. I woke up to the sound of the showers running in the training house and began my morning yoga. The students had to wait before stepping on the monastery grounds until 5 or so, and only then could they go straight to the temple to wait for roll call.

Our work week was usually five days long depending on certain calendar exceptions that sometimes made the week four or six days long. Our weekend was normally two days but once a month had three days of non-department work. It was rare to have a full day off. Most of the young to middle-aged monks had at least half a day of work to accomplish on a "weekend." Sometimes it was cooking, other times it would be an obligation to travel to town. Also, travel was always done with another monk since we never traveled alone, always in pairs.

The temple was built by the monks in the 1970s, brick by brick and beam by beam. The large granite threshold in the doorway is two feet thick and blocked anyone from casually entering the sacred room. The stone floor beam made you aware that you were walking into a special room designed for a specific purpose. Your feet landed on fluffy, lavender carpet that covered the entire floor where the public were allowed to sit. The temple walls were four feet thick, two feet of CMU block on the inside covered by two feet of stone on the outside. The ceiling rafters were all beautiful redwood beams wrapped in dust and smoke from the weekly *homa* fires.

Siva was and is the main Godhead and creator worshipped at Kauai's Hindu Monastery. Our day began with 30 minutes of ceremony called *puja* directly after roll call. Seating was always on the floor and in order of rank. The monks always sat, stood, spoke and even drove in order of rank. The youngest ones were always "seen but not heard" and were expected to look and act their best as they represented the monastery.

After Siva puja, the monks gathered for a one-hour meditation in another part of the temple called the *Guru Pitham*. The Pitham had a thin, wooden, sliding door that connected it to the temple. One would have to turn sideways in order to get from one room to another and if you faced too far to the front your shoulders stopped you from fitting. The thin door was akin to the temple's threshold, it was an expression of the room you were about to enter: built for a special and specific purpose.

Our morning meditations were always guided by a senior monk, conducted in the language of *Shum*. Shum was created and developed by my paramaguru (the guru of my guru), Satguru Sivaya Subramuniyaswami, in the late 1960s while on a group travel-study program in Switzerland. At the time of this writing, Shum has 174 characters, each one with a symbol and color that can be used as a meditation on focus and concentration.

I should note here that it takes almost two years to become a monk under vows. Before then the students are only allowed to study with an older monk, not meditate with the group. Our class of students would sit in a semicircle around the monk teaching at 6am, while the group of monks did their practice in the other part of the temple. One symbol and color at a time, we slowly learned and memorized the language of Shum and practiced using it in meditations for our small group.

Do not defend your ego.

A monk is trained to surrender and not defend oneself in order to look better. The continual practice of not "saving face" was training me to be completely free and powerful.

One of the most ineffective strategies for harmonious survival, whether in a relationship or professional team, is to try and defend the way you appear to others, also known as saving face. Saving face is defined as "avoiding humiliation or embarrassment, to maintain dignity or preserve reputation," and it could cost you your relationship or job if taken to extremes.

The greatest leaders throughout history took the blame, and leaders in high positions continue to do so. Why? Imagine you are the boss for once; imagine that you need to find out what is going on in one of your departments or teams or chains. Which would be easier to work with: a team that pointed the finger at others or circumstances, or a team member that was open and honest, declaring they would take the blame and create a solution? Obviously, the team member that steps up and says they will take charge is going to make your job as a boss easier, and that's how we want our boss to feel: like we are responsible for their rice bowl.

A rice bowl is someone's livelihood in business; we don't play around with that or else we pay the consequences. Instead, we nurture relationships, take blame, resolve to fix, cooperate, support and work together. We don't lie inside the team dynamic; we don't report behind backs and destroy interpersonal relationships. We confront; we remain open; we apologize and we admit when we don't know or need help. Simple. Stop making yourself look better and start putting the face of the team in the forefront. That helps your boss look good and that is what's important.

* * *

Most of the monks had a free hour before morning meetings started at 8am. For me that meant foraging the lush monastery grounds for tropical fruit. The monks had 51 acres of papaya, citrus (orange, grapefruit, lime and lemon), palm, coconut, guava, and jackfruit trees. Some areas grew exotic sweets like chikku, rambutan, durian, and lychee that I'd stroll to in my white robes and pick at my leisure. What a joy it was to pick and eat at will! I remember the ripest chikku tasted like maple syrup.

The monks in charge of the milking used that hour to squeeze the dairy cows of milk, and drive back to the main building to store the product in the large walk-in fridge. Others tended to the fish, cats, cobwebs and small areas they were responsible for keeping up. A monk was responsible for a lot of little things, mostly cleaning, and the way he cared for his duties was a reflection of his mind. Was he clean or cluttered? Does his desk look sloppy? Or, is everything right where it should be? The outer mind showed clearly what was going on inside the monk's being and if meditation was being performed correctly.

Each department had a different 8am team meeting. The media department, GK, made sure to meet every morning since they were in charge of the editorials and blog for the monastery. Each meeting lasted roughly one hour and covered current events and FYIs, which were important to voice in the GK so every aspect of the day's work could be on point and everyone was informed about everyone else's workload.

The accounting department, PK, met at a more convenient time for all the members since their jobs were more spread out. Their meetings lasted no more than 15 minutes since nothing in accounting was urgent.

In the landscaping and construction department, SK, the meetings were similar to the GK since the department head had been trained there as a young monk. He took after his mentor and made sure his SK team was of the same high standard. Work orders, urgent repairs and large purchases were all covered on a daily basis.

The LK and EK, temple and church membership respectively, combined their teams into one and covered all the topics regarding special guests and pilgrims, upcoming festivals and holidays, the week's astrology and bulk food orders for the three-month supply. Since the monastery was on a small island plagued by hurricanes, the dry food supply was always topped up to last three months. During my stay of 12 years I never experienced any major storm or hurricane.

The daily morning department reports were given according to rank, the most senior speaking first and the most junior (sometimes that meant visiting guests) speaking last. To speak out of turn was looked down upon, and a senior would interrupt and remind you to wait your turn. It was during the morning reports that I got the first taste of subordination and patience in my life, and it felt good once I got the hang of it. One of the first meetings I participated in was for the landscaping department. The senior would perform a short *arati* (waving of a lit lamp) to the department's deity, and then began chanting the mantra for it. After the short opening ceremony that each day's meeting started with, the group then began the department affirmation. Each department had an affirmation, or spoken mission statement, proclaiming what we as monks believed in, and what the group's focus was to be. The structure was something that I had never experienced before, and it became clear to me that the discipline and structure from those meetings was why the work went on so well, and that each company or group with a centralized focus does need an affirmation or mission statement and should refer to it daily.

The same rank rule applied to lunch, both sitting and speaking. After working the morning shift from 8am to 12:30pm, the monks would then clean a specific area to which they were assigned for 30 minutes. Lunch gathered in a small courtyard at exactly 1:08pm. Everyone gathered their lunch, buffet-style served in a room connected to the kitchen called the Java Cafe and headed through an outdoor corridor to the courtyard. The monks sat carefully on mats to shield the hard red brick floor from their clean robes and ate lunch in silence until the guru asked to hear the day's report.

Each day had a different report from one of the five departments. Again, the monks spoke in order of seniority, and the department even had a rank for the given day. The highest ranking department spoke on the first day of the week, while the most junior spoke on the last. Inside the monastery, there was always a microcosmic world, or rule structure, surrounding the macrocosm. From the outside, an observer may think a department is speaking on a random occasion but there is a specific reason, schedule and plan to everything that went on inside the monastery, and it all reflected the order one is supposed to hold inside themselves. If this kind of structure is not present inside the individual, we would teach, then one cannot meditate to the standard of monks—and the mind will be too hard to control.

Never stop reading.

We cannot learn enough from our own experience. It's far too short and slow going to learn that much but there's a solution. When we read biography, autobiography, history, philosophy and some fiction (I don't recommend a lot of fiction since it tends to be more abstract and life lessons could be harder to grasp) we enrich our mind with the experience of others. Their perspective on life helps us see ours in a wider, less myopic view. The struggles and pains of history are often the greatest gems we can grasp from reading.

Learning what has come before can give us insight into why we do what we do (learning is mostly from imitating our parents), and what we should do in any given situation. Culture and tradition stays afloat on the ocean of the written word; ethics and morals all passed down from storytelling can continue to broaden our way of thinking—assuming we do a great deal of thinking.

This aphorism is as much advice as it is a warning: keep educating yourself or the mind will grow stale and your view of life will shrink until all you remember is that which occurs only at your work and home life.

* * *

After lunch, most of the monks enjoyed an afternoon siesta. Even a young, spry fellow like myself enjoyed them for several years into my training. (It wasn't until my 4th or 5th year of monastic life that I used that time to train in the gym or run the grounds seeking elite physical fitness.) For the young students, we didn't have much of a choice; we had to be off the property for that time. We were encouraged to study books, meditation or practice our hatha yoga postures. All the monks had to learn a set of 24 postures or *asanas* in order to complete basic training with good marks. The end result was to sit in full lotus, or *padmasana*, posture for the duration of the hour-long meditation.

I had grown fond of the yoga system developed by the monks, and I practiced after lunch and in the evening, before my meditation. (I eventually developed a repetitive strain injury in my knee, forcing me to reduce my practice to once a day.) Instead of going back to our assigned department at 3pm, the students left the house and walked across a field to the main temple, Kadavul Hindu Temple, and worshipped at the 3pm service to Lord Ganesha. After the ceremony, we all gathered in the Guru Pitham for a class with one of the senior monks. Classes varied from philosophy to hatha yoga instruction. On a special occasion, we would have class with the guru of the monastery, Satguru Bodhinatha Veylanswami.

We returned to our department late, around 4 or 4:30pm, and worked until 6pm. All the monks were off then and were allowed to relax, help other monks on projects, exercise or head to bed early if they had to wake up for a midnight or 3am temple shift. The students were allowed to roam the property and visit the temple one last time before packing up dinner at 6:30pm and head to the training house. Some days I roamed, others I meditated in the temple, everyone gathered at the training house and sat around to hang out. We were young men all around the same age so we grew to be friends. All of us were there for the same reason, to master meditation and explore Hinduism as a monk. There was no question at that point, we knew what we wanted and would dedicate our lives in search of the mystery that lay within us.

I did well on the six-month Taskforce program. My meditation skills were increasing exponentially by the day and life had new meaning. *I did it*, I would think to myself, *I finally found what I was supposed to do with my life.* The concept of monastic life was simple: dedicate your whole being to the search for the greater Self inside each of us. The work I did, however mundane (washing the monastery utility vehicles was a big one), was actually bringing me joy. I sang religious songs; cared for the earth; dug my feet into the soil; and planted food in the gardens. Everything seemed to fit into place just as it should.

Eventually, people would come and go in the student training house, and after three months, I had the place to myself. When young men did show up, I was the house senior and could answer questions and feel important. My mind was settled and made up by the end of the training period. I was to go home for a minimum of three months and decide if I wanted to return. For the months I would be home, my mission was to settle debts, tell family and friends my plans, and legally change my name. A plane ticket was bought for me; I said my goodbyes and was off back to the world that I left.

My mother was living in Indiana at the time (she later would move to Texas), and I stayed with her throughout the transition. I started the name-change process right away. Indiana law (2007) required that I get a lawyer for my name change and publish the request in the local newspaper for three weeks. While awaiting the court date to officially have a judge change my name I worked with Sam, my friend and comrade who got the asphalt business just six months prior, and was able to earn some money in order to pay off the few debts I had.

My court date finally arrived and I appeared before an Indiana judge to change my legal name. This wasn't the first time I was in a courtroom; so I felt right at home. By now I figured out how to act, speak, and keep a respectable appearance. Before the monastery, I had been before judges to deal with community service, drug arrests, and traffic violations. Back then I was rude, young, and somehow better than everyone else. Now that I had a higher purpose I treated people with respect and gave them full attention when they spoke and said little.

"Come on in, the judge is ready to see you," said the bailiff.

I walked in the small courtroom and stood next to my lawyer. She greeted me with a smile and assured me it would only take a few minutes.

"Next case, please," said the judge softly. She was a large woman who was ready for someone to finally be calm and just listen for once without arguing.

"Your honor, my client would like to change his legal name from Joseph Houston Chikiar to Rajan Shankara as he is converting to Hinduism and going to be a monk in a monastery."

The judge removed her large glasses and looked at me directly in the eyes and asked, "Son, you want to change your name to Rajan Shankara and move to a monastery in Hawaii?"

"Yes, ma'am," I said with confidence, "that's correct."

The judge put her glasses back on with a big smile across her face, raised her gavel in the air and said, "Have a nice life," before yelling, "NEXT."

A good leader will work hard to empower everyone around them.

The term servant leader sums up this aphorism but it isn't self-evident what that means. A leader needs to not only make sure they take the blame but must also make everyone around them better than they are. Those qualities surrounding the team's capability for work: critical thinking, ability to anticipate, efficiency, and planning should be a part of everyone's job description, not just the leader's. It's not wrong for a leader to be ignorant of every detail in an operation, and it is ineffective for a leader to attempt to overpower their team and pretend that they can do everything better—which is simply not possible.

A wise leader understands that they don't have a choice about their team; they can either empower the group to accomplish their work better than their own abilities allow or they can become ineffective as a whole and accomplish far less. Why aren't more teams and leaders involved in this kind of effort? Fear. There is still plenty of fear-based leadership going on. Fear of giving someone responsibility, fear of mistakes, fear of overspending. If the leader has got it in their mind that they can do the job better, then the team has been truncated or alienated, and will often reflect that in their work or attitude.

Give people the power, trust, and resources they need to succeed and they will surprise you.

* * *

To whom it may concern, this letter is about the outstanding bill for Joseph Houston Chikiar. My name is now Rajan Shankara, formerly known as Joseph Houston Chikiar, and I've just returned from living in a monastery for six months. I have decided to become a monk and live a spiritual life dedicated to the service of my Hindu religion and for its followers. I have no money and make no money and am soon to return to the Hawaiian monastery again to stay for the rest of my life. I hope you understand and find some way to help me with my debt to the hospital. Thank you for your time.

The letter above was written when I first got back to the mainland in hopes of having my debt cleared due to my unusual circumstances. Working with Sam helped pay one of my two debts, one with an ambulance company I needed in the past, but the second was a hospital debt that still had to be taken care of—and far too large for me to afford. Weeks later, an official statement from the hospital arrived at my mother's mailbox.

Dear Rajan Shankara, the hospital has received your letter asking for help regarding your outstanding bill. We understand you have decided to join a monastery and dedicated your life to a religious path, earning no income and helping others. The hospital has decided to remove your debt so that you may return to your work in Hawaii.

It wasn't until months later and recounting the story to another monk that I realized how unusual the events of my life really were, for me anyways. Perhaps it is normal for hospitals to write letters like that but I certainly hadn't heard of it before in my small circle. Not only was I given a second chance at freedom from my run-in with the law but a large debt had been wiped clean, and I was able to be reborn. The person I used to be was fading away and a new, more disciplined man was coming into the world for the first time.

The weeks went by slowly as I waited out the three-month minimum before I could return. I wasted time by biking to my friend Adam's house in Park Forest, Illinois. He would go to work and I played his guitar and wrote poetry, a typical bum.

I had nothing to do and didn't want to be out in the world anyway. Sure, looking back I could have spent my time helping others, giving back, donating my time to something valuable and enriching, but I didn't. I was ready to leave the world and renounce, I was ready for my robes and beads. I didn't even spend more time with family. Instead, I wasted away with friends and knew that I wasn't long for the world. I was living in an actual "… if you only had three months to live…" scenario and acted as if I was already dead.

I got a phone call from one of the monks one afternoon while meditating on my mother's porch.

"Are you ready to come back?" the monk said with that calming tone all the Hawaiian monks carried.

I attempted to hide my excitement, "Yes, absolutely. When do I fly?"

Challenge, pain and hardship bring about our character from within.

The revolutionary hero is the individual who decides voluntarily, courageously, to face some aspect of the still-unknown and threatening.
Dr. Jordan B. Peterson, *Maps of Meaning*

There is an odd truth to life: only when we experience pain and challenge can we know who we really are. Without a test of will, we simply won't make enough of an effort to make lasting changes to our being. Without hardship, we really will never know just how much we can endure and just how powerful we are. If everything was given to us and made simple, we wouldn't appreciate it.

Carrying a burden takes away your uniqueness and unifies you with every other human. One such example is that of the mythological Greek king Sisyphus. Punished to an eternal relationship with a hill and a massive rock, Sisyphus was forced to push the rock up a hill only to have the rock never reach the top and forever roll down again. The conscious observation of his own suffering allowed the Greek king to keep going, and some imagine he did it with a smile on his face. Knowing that we all carry our own Sisyphean rock helps to alleviate the thought of our painful existence. Believing that the rock is actually why we were born in the first place, and knowing that our mission consists of pushing that rock, or carrying the burden, gives us a reason to keep pushing—else we let go, the rock comes down on us and crushes our meaning and purpose.

It's often this principle that has given my clients the most relief. It gives us a "why" to all the madness that surrounds us. As religious author Robert Elliott Speer once wrote, "no strong man was ever made without resistance." It is the very resistance of life, or our endeavors, or those that surround us that cause suffering in the first place. The ability to face our life wherever it is, and to face the people and situations within it, is the grist mill for our soul's evolution. Without challenge, pain, or hardship there would never be any act worthy of praise or anything worth doing at all.

> And so it is hard to be good, for surely hard it is in each instance to find the mean, just as to find the mean point or centre of a circle is not what any man can do, but only he who knows how: just so to be angry, to give money, and be expensive, is what any man can do, and easy: but to do these to the right person, in due proportion, at the right time, with a right object, and in the right manner, this is not as before what any man can do, nor is it easy; and for this cause goodness is rare, and praiseworthy, and noble.
> Aristotle, *Nicomachean Ethics*

* * *

My ticket was purchased by the monastery, and it was now a matter of days till I returned to the island of Kauai. I did my rounds and visited close friends to give my farewells, and I spent more time with family than before. This time around I was a much different person, and I understood that I might not be returning home. The feeling of returning to the first place that I felt meaning and purpose—and truly feeling like myself—was surreal.

I was picked up at the airport by a man named Deva Rajan and his wife Gayatri. Deva was a tall, thin and elegant-looking man who dressed simply. His wife Gayatri was much shorter, but wore a smile on her face that could illuminate any dark corner on this Earth. As we drove up the long winding road to the monastery, Deva tried to give me an update on what I missed, what day it was on the lunar calendar, and anything else I needed to feel informed about. He and Gayatri were so sweet and welcoming, and I had the feeling of familiarity, as if I was meeting long-lost parents.

As I closed the car door behind me Deva assured me, "If there's anything you need, feel free to ask us!"

Not long after his, Gayatri womped him on the shoulder proclaiming, "OH, he can ask the monks if he needs anything!"

I walked up the entryway into the training house feeling loved and cared for.

I arrived on a "retreat day," one of two weekend days for the monks, and so the other young gents were able to greet me at the house. They showed me to my sleeping arrangements and let me get settled in. I had a pair of work clothes, town clothes and a full set of robes waiting for me. Everyone took turns explaining how they liked to wear them and what was proper attire for temple and leisure. I never once got the sense of being overwhelmed. This was it. I had found my calling and changed into my new robes as if I was changing the skin of my body. Nothing felt awkward or new, everything felt just as it should.

The next day was the beginning of the week known as "Sun 1"; so, I didn't do much but go to the temple and pay my respects. A Hindu temple has an interesting feel to it, almost as if you are saying to the deity, "I'm here!" and all of the inner-world beings hover around the newcomer with delight. At least, that's how it felt to me.

The training house looked like it was built in the 60s. The interior design was simple, mostly open with wooden floors and a few shag carpets. The wood floor squeaked so badly that no one could take a step without sending a slight shiver down your neck. No food was kept in the house and the bathrooms appeared as if no one used them. That's how we were trained, of course. Each monk was meant to live as though he were not there and could travel at a moment's notice. Living the lifestyle of a ghost makes it easy to study and eventually master the mind. Mastering the mind meant conquering meditation. Each bed was neatly folded as if no one had slept in it the night before, and the dining room table appeared to have never been used. These boys were sharp, clean and strict, and they left a massive impression on me the moment I arrived. They spoke with intention and as if a senior was watching, but they had love and care in their voices and demeanor.

The next morning started with roll call in the temple at 5:30am and I could hardly sleep I was so full of wonder and awe. I got up early along with another named Robin around 4am. We did yoga, prepared our robes, and drank tea. I had been the newest of the full house, so everyone else had their own rooms while I was on the couch. Some of the guys didn't leave their rooms until roll call, but being on the couch meant I was up when the earliest riser got up to shower. I so enjoyed those early hour moments when nothing outside was alive, and the inside of the house was so still you could see the unmoved air floating before you.

Once showered and properly in uniform, the guys would open the stiff sliding wooden door and walk through the backyard to the monastery trail that led down to the temple. We tended to walk as a group since we were still guests, and showing up alone felt like it had an air of pretension.

Ask constantly: Who am I? What am I all about? How much can I endure?

There's much to be written about these three questions. Finding out who we are, what we stand for and how much pain can we tolerate should be something children are taught, and it's possible they are to a degree. But the answer to these questions lies in deep self-reflection and constant introspection. But once the pains of introspection are solidified with habit, and we've gotten past the trauma of our parents and upbringing, we can begin to reap the benefits of innate knowledge.

Who Are You? Well, who are you? Are you something that changes—emotionally, spiritually, physically—every time the wind blows? Or are you rooted and anchored in a personal knowing of who you really are? Not many people know the answer to that question, nor have they ever given it any thought. "Well, I'm Jack DeVille and I live in Connecticut and I have a wife and three dogs... so, yeah, I know who I am." But are you Jack in Connecticut? What happens if Connecticut goes away? Or what happens when your dogs die, you get a divorce and lose everything? Are you still Jack with things? Or what about when you die? What are you then?

There has to be an undying presence that exists inside you, all around you, that is you. There needs to be an identification change, a change from that which is temporary to that which has always been and will always be. Once we can identify with that, we can begin to sustain a sense of contentment no matter what goes on around or inside us.

What are you all about? Well, what the hell do you stand for? There's got to be some kind of internalized principle in that spirit of yours. When all is said and done, your clothes are stripped away, and you can no longer hide behind those sunglasses, you're going to need something you stand for. We call these morals, and they used to be passed down from father to son, mother to daughter and wisemen to the village. But, in today's world, we don't have mentors who can guide us; we have celebrity figures explaining their views on social media, and we latch onto the latest trend because why the hell not. But it's bullshit.

You've got to know what you stand for when someone puts a gun to your head. What are you willing to die for? How many pushups can you do? Every man should know that. Would you hunt and kill for food if you had to? Would you defend your town, city, state, or country if it came down to it? Or are you hoping that never happens? Are you coasting through your job, not wanting to create any conflict, just wishing everyone would ignore you so that you can just get back home without making a sound?

Find something to stand for because the alternative means you won't be able to hold a conversation long enough to produce any change whatsoever.

Innate knowledge is that which emanates from within you. It's the "ah ha" moments, the intuition coming from a long walk alone, or the spontaneous recall of a word or memory we called upon in a time before. Introspection—looking within—is the act of researching our own mind in order to withdraw the knowledge it already contains. By unlocking the storehouse of information our mind and souls contain, we are better able to serve ourselves as well as those around us, and anyone who comes across our path.

Endure. If life had to be summed up in one word it would be Endure. If it had to be two words it would be Endure Suffering. We're all here to experience that which will change us, make us evolve, and keep expanding our consciousness enough until we don't need to focus on it so much; then, we can finally start helping out on a large scale. It's not a question of whether you will have to go through challenge and hardship, but *how much?*

Enduring then becomes a game-like-challenge to be conquered. As leaders, we can anticipate challenges and show others how to endure as we come up with solutions (or delegate appropriately to others) which keeps everything flowing smoothly. Once this becomes a pattern, we become effective, powerful people who increase our circle of influence, and voice the needed opinion for the company or team surrounding us.

* * *

After the *homa* (fire ceremony) that starts off every work week, I approached the monk who managed my entrance into the program. He is a tall, slender, and kind man with a patchy brown beard and bright blue eyes with naturally curling eyelashes that are inviting and sweet.

"Welcome! You made it back," he said with a soft and nurturing voice.

"Yes! Thank you so much for your help, swami. Which department will I serve in?"

My question was not without trepidation. Upon return to the monastery, I was to be assigned a department that I would serve for the rest of my life. One could petition a change of service, but it was rare and seen as worldly. While I was in the air flying across the ocean, the elders would have had a meeting deciding my fate. Whichever area of service I did best in while I was on the Taskforce program, would be the department I was sent to.

The tall swami (monk) standing next to Saravananathaswami bent forward in order for our eyes to meet and almost whispered, "You will be with me and my team, welcome."

The monk speaking was named Yoginathaswami and I had spent extra time in his SK, the department in charge of the grounds, building maintenance, construction, organic gardening and farming.

"Excellent!" I said a little too loudly as the temple attendees turned slightly from the deity to my conversation. "When do I start, swami?" I asked with child-like enthusiasm.

"You start today. Our team coordination meeting is in 15 minutes… you didn't forget, did you? You weren't away that long!" said swami with a giant laugh that shook his robes. Yoginathaswami was 6 foot 4 inches tall and had to look down whenever he wished to speak to someone in order to meet their eyes. A truly gentle giant with passion for whatever he was involved with.

My initial training began with basic grunt work, grinding the rust off metal mowers, pressure-washing sidewalks, painting, fueling the vehicles and learning how to be a shadow to whom I was helping. My training was not based on learning a trade but understanding the artisan/apprentice concept. Being a good subordinate and being able to anticipate the needs of my artisan was essential to a harmonious department and having a one-mind workflow.

Up to this point in my life, I had always been a big-headed know-it-all who didn't take orders too well. Having the grace of formality and novelty worked well for several months, but then I started to have my own ideas and share them freely. Slowly, I regressed to my former self and started to stand out in ways a good monk would not.

The path to taking monastic vows is almost two years long. At this stage of my journey, I was no longer a taskforcer as we called it but an *aspirant*. I was at a stage where expectations grew higher, and I could now be faulted for incorrect behavior and attitudes. This stage takes another six months to complete before becoming a *supplicant*, and that lasts for another six to nine months depending on the ability to complete certain written requirements and tests. The completion of supplicancy makes one a *postulant*, or full-fledged monk. The rank for that level of lay monk is called *Sadhaka*, or seeker. Seekers wear white and continue to shave the head and face every day. The postulant monk, sadhaka, wears white for at least three years before donning the yellow waist sash and becoming a *Natyam*, or dancer, a sign that one has done well and is approved by the elders to one day become a *Yogi* rank and wear full yellow robes. Those yellow robes must be worn for at least two years and a maximum of eight. If the Yogi rank goes past eight years then the monk is demoted to wearing white until the age of 72, a sign that he has not yet matured into representing the monastery to the public.

The mission was to earn the respect of everyone around you and receive the yellow sash as a Natyam. Performance reviews were not uncommon, and one knew that your rapport with your department head was essential to getting good marks with the elders. The ranking system was designed to show stages of outer and inner growth. Our colors and titles were clear indicators of what kind of person one was dealing with and the information they contained. While no one stated outright that they wanted the yellow sash of the Natyam, we all knew it to be implicit.

Section 3: Meditation

Meditation is not the first step in self-discovery; understanding the mind is.

In the field of meditation there are many charlatans. Yogis of all kinds will expound on the benefits of meditation, and they will want you to begin with their practice immediately. Meditation is a road that has many switchbacks and will show you the darkest corners of your mind—it is not for everyone. The steps before meditation are more external, like cleaning the dirt, debris and grit off a car before it can be waxed and polished. Inside the mind there are many issues yet to be resolved such as past trauma, experiences we can't get over, and confusions revolving around people and things. Before meditation is fruit-bearing, one needs to first resolve that which has caused any disturbance, and it usually revolves around our past. In this way, trauma and pain won't appear in the mind of the meditator to be stronger and more vivid than if it were happening in the flesh.

Why should we be so cautious about meditation? Isn't it just breathing and relaxing? One of the biggest misconceptions about meditation is that it's just breathing and relaxing. This is wrong. Breathing and relaxing are actually just two aspects of paying attention, otherwise known as being mindful or being observant. Sitting, breathing, relaxing, as well as becoming aware of the body (and the life force running through your veins) are the initial steps leading you into concentration, and then into meditation.

In my Yogi training, at one of the world's foremost institutions on meditation, highly trained Yogis don't even meditate for almost two years. We were taught to prepare; to master the initial stages of attention and concentration first; then, slowly enter into the realms of meditation and contemplation using techniques developed specifically for monks. If you sit daily and relax, watch your breathing and lower your blood pressure—

congrats, I am happy for you—but make no mistake, your journey into meditation has only just begun.

Understanding the mind is crucial to resolving past trauma, moving forward with being comfortable in our own skin, being in loving relationships, and being the most effective person in our professional work. We can break the mind down to three main areas: instinctive, intellectual and intuitive.

Instinctive areas include things like digestion, basic cravings of hunger, the emotional systems that work with the physical body. These things happen automatically, meaning we don't have to think about blood flow, it just happens on its own.

The intellectual area of the mind is both a natural summation of previous knowledge accrued over time and also something we cultivate throughout life as we collect data from interacting with the world, in our experience. Humans rarely turn inward and reflect on what's going on inside—where the intellect comes from—so we think the intellect is book knowledge only.

Third, is the intuitive area of the mind also called the superconscious area. It deals with the higher part of us, the moments of deep reflection, intuition, and love for those around us without judgment or reason. When our energy is spent in this area, we are regularly on time for everything, we consistently have those great days, we're in control of our feelings, and everyone and everything around us just clicks. Creativity comes out of us from this area as well. Hopefully, we all know what that feels like.

The instinctive mind is our survival instinct, self-preservation—where hunger and thirst are born—and should not be feared or thought of as brute. We don't have to give all of our energy to it since that would take us out of balance, but we should cultivate what it feels like to be instinctive, animalistic, and masculine as well as how to go in and out of it, when appropriate. What comes out of this area are the base emotions of fear, greed, hatred, anger, lust and jealousy. Those are all instinctive forces. They are very real and we all know what acting with those traits feels like, but we can rarely control them. When we can't control our instinctive nature we become erratic creatures and without reason. We are not conscious of this since it happens instinctively. This is the fight or flight reflex as well. In a moment of emergency, the instinctive mind can take over and guide us on how to act next.

For our sanity and for our general peace of mind and wellness in life, we want to express ourselves through the other two areas of the mind, the intellectual and intuitive/superconscious. It's within these two areas that we better ourselves and our situation tremendously. We create by writing, painting, producing music, teaching, reflecting. We do this by observation of life around us and by observing ourselves. The intellectual and intuitive minds thrive on observation—being aware of what's going on around you. If we are not consciously aware, we could lose our sense of the higher faculties and resort back to instinct-driven attitudes that have little use to most situations. When well-trained, we can use the instinctive part of us and react with intelligence and with love at the same time. We can have a greater insight into a situation and no longer resort to anger or irrational arguments, which lead to saying or doing something we later regret. The instinct is powerful and when it is under our control we find humans able to better understand their own natures, proclivities, weaknesses, and strengths.

* * *

As soon as I got into the rhythm of work and worship, my argumentative side came to light. I felt like I knew better in some scenarios, even when I didn't have the experience to back it up. One of the monastery's techniques for resolving confrontations was to stop work, sit down, and talk it out. Both sides were allowed to express how they felt about the situation and, ideally, a resolution came which resulted in the two monks being harmonious again. The hard rule was that the situation had to be resolved in some way before going to sleep, that meant conversing throughout the night to reach a conclusion both agreed upon. And yes, I started to have my share of sit-downs with the team I worked with.

I remember being emotional at work, sitting down on the job, speaking out of turn, reworking plans without approval, and thinking I was incredibly efficient when I wasn't. I'd stepped full-blown into my old, egotistical, asshole personae. Over the months (a few years in total), I was corrected by everyone I worked with and had an argumentative nature that was difficult to train. One of my seniors reported my leadership skills as "mean" on a performance review, and I was. I lacked the skills to be harmonious with others and I was deficient in work productivity, basic trade skills, communication and efficiency; yet, in my mind I was amazing, quick, intelligent and top dog. I was a narcissist.

With all of the meditation, physical labor, and educational classes I went through, there was a breaking point where my body would catch up to all of the growth and development that my mind was going through. I, eventually, had what I am calling a nervous system restructuring, alteration, and breakdown. The person I had been could no longer deny the transformation happening to my mind and the maturity taking place so quickly. This is mystically known as the grace of the guru, and it arrives spontaneously and it is quite painful. It is the dissolution of the former self, to the new more improved person. It is beyond the normal character and attitude shift, and even beyond a new paradigm or worldview adjustment. What begins to happen is that an entirely new person is being born out of right thought, right knowledge, and right action.

Our previous selves are ruled by the ego. The slow and painful deconstruction and, later, disillusionment of that ego-driven self is a type of death experience. Once the ego learns that a greater force is trying to take over the operating system, it will do whatever it takes to stop the coup—even if it results in permanent damage or alteration to the host. This was not the only ego death for me, but it was the first ego-altering experience that I needed for the next and final experience to be permanent. The transformation of who I was and how I viewed my reality to the new and capable, ever-evolving character was beginning to take place, and no one around me would say exactly what was going on.

My first, major alteration of self was on what seemed to be a normal day as I was left to do my work, while my department head and his second-in-command drove into town to get parts for one of the tractors. I had the job of grinding a trailer tongue down to its bare metal and coating it with a metal protectant and sealant which was easy enough. The job required no real skill except for holding onto a brush cup grinder upside down and dealing with shards of metal debris getting in your eyes. Typical grunt work for my department but a good, thorough job was always expected. It was on this day that I felt particularly creative and wanted to do a good job so everyone was impressed. The grinder was my paintbrush and the trailer tongue was my canvas. I was going to do the finest grind and paint the department, and my boss, had ever seen and be rewarded... I was sure of it.

Three hours later the trailer tongue held a stunning, glossy, black finish that made it look brand new, and it would make anyone think twice about towing the trailer ever again for fear of scratching that tongue. My department head returned from town just as I was finishing the job and, boy, was I proud. I was ready for the garlands to be wrapped around my neck and a promotion waiting for me. This was one of the first, manual-labor jobs I genuinely cared about. The moment of truth came and my boss walked by and looked at my work.

"Nice work," he said, "you're just finishing now?"

"Yes, sir!" I said proudly. "Just over three hours of work. All done."

"Come inside," my boss said and walked away knowing I would follow.

I sat down in his office and was ready for my pats on the back, but the scolding that followed was something I never saw coming.

"How can something so simple take you three hours to complete? We'll never be able to accomplish our mission if every job took all morning. This is unacceptable!"

I was crushed and beyond defeated. I felt like I had zero worth as my visions of grandeur came crashing down on top of me. The power in which his words hit me were like arrows going straight into my heart. After a few moments of silence, the ego and self-transformation began. All of a sudden, my fingers stuck together as if glue were in between them; my fists clamped down and crimped themselves inward; and tears poured out of my eyes and rolled down my face. In a matter of minutes, I had been reduced to a child.

"What's wrong with you, boy?!" my boss questioned, which I myself was also wondering. I was still fully conscious and aware of what was going on, internally coherent, but externally I no longer had control. My body regressed into childhood and I continued to cry, cramp, and curl up into a ball as I sat in a chair next to my boss's desk. My ego was fighting back while my intelligence tried to absorb the lesson. It was literally crying out for air in hopes of saving face while my conscious mind knew my department head had every right to correct my work. The ego, my ego, was so strong, and up to this point unchallenged, that it had had enough.

My senior also had enough and could watch this peril no more. He grabbed my shoulders and pulled me up saying, "Come on, we're going for a walk." And so we headed out of the office and down a jungle path that was more secluded. My crying got louder; my hands crimped in on themselves so much they began to hurt; and my body was ill. I was able to sneak a few words out, and ask for help to undo my hand grip. He grabbed my hands and manually opened them up as if he was unwinding the tension of a bench vice. I could now walk and use my arms normally, but the tears kept coming as a part of me died.

In the same moment, we walked past my guru and I immediately felt ashamed. I looked to the ground for solace and he jokingly said to my boss, "You know something is wrong when the SK is walking." Our department almost never walked the grounds during work hours, but drove the Kawasaki 4x4 Mule vehicles about the property.

We walked for a good hour until I regained strength and came to. I was given the rest of the day off and would return to work the next day. I was never the same after that breakdown, and the department head and I never spoke about it to anyone, even ourselves.

We can control fear, anxiety, frustration and anger with meditative practices. We don't have to live inside anyone else.

We experience sorrow and pain when our awareness latches onto everything around us. That could mean attaching onto different things such as: our life situations, people and their emotions, objects and our desire to hold onto and not ever lose them, and the pressure that comes from the unexpected, unplanned, and unknown areas of our existence. That attachment is fueled by your body's energy system. Practicing detachment, dispassion, observation, attention, concentration and meditation allows you to control where the body's energy goes and how it is used. Your energy is also your awareness; your awareness is also your consciousness. You are your own unlimited energy source.

If we wish to control our mind, we must begin to harness the energy that runs through it—that's where awareness or consciousness comes in. It is actually our awareness, or our lens of reality, that reveals to us our mental pictures, thoughts, and feelings. If we control awareness, then we take hold of the force that powers our mind. We do that by realizing the mind is a separate entity, understanding we are in control of it, and practicing that control. Practice is twofold. First, we train our ability to direct breathing consciously, followed by consciously directing our awareness. Second, we direct our awareness using the three Ds of energy management: discrimination, detachment, and dispassion. After enough practice, perhaps as little as a few weeks, our minds become calm as if it is a leashed animal waiting for our command.

* * *

I distinctly remember a change in my attitude and character as well as the way I viewed seniority. It began from the nervous breakdown onward. It wasn't long after that I was introduced to the ideas and philosophy of Stephen Covey, the motivational speaker that covered topics on making people highly effective. I don't know why exactly, but his 1979 audio lecture series of his *7 Habits* furthered my development and maturation like nothing before. Why was this all happening now? Could I have understood the same teachings as my former self? Chances are I wouldn't have been receptive to them. My mind and body had undergone an alteration that allowed new teachings to enter and actually allow me to absorb them. I was now addicted to self-help, self-motivation, and self-reliance.

I continued my studies over the coming years and relied on the teachings of the Stoics: Epictetus, Marcus Aurelius, and Seneca; religious authors such as Robert Elliott Speer; philosophers Socrates, Plato and Aristotle; autobiography and biography of notable figures from history; military strategy accounts from soldiers; Buddhist and Zen texts; and I got into the darker sides of war by reading about POW accounts and slavery. The amount of knowledge I took in was unending; I needed it like I needed air to breathe.

One of the profound works that stood out to me was *Walden* by Henry David Thoreau. I simply never encountered such a rich view of life before, especially—in Thoreau's case—a life of minimalism and asceticism. I'll never forget his reasoning for living in a self-made, wooden shack for two years,

> I went to the woods because I wished to live deliberately, to front only the essential facts of life, and see if I could not learn what it had to teach, and not, when I came to die, discover that I had not lived. I did not wish to live what was not life, living is so dear; nor did I wish to practice resignation, unless it was quite necessary. I wanted to live deep and suck out

all the marrow of life, to live so sturdily and Spartan-like as to put to rout all that was not life, to cut a broad swath and shave close, to drive life into a corner, and reduce it to its lowest terms, and, if it proved to be mean, why then to get the whole and genuine meanness of it, and publish its meanness to the world; or if it were sublime, to know it by experience, and be able to give a true account of it in my next excursion. For most men, it appears to me, are in a strange uncertainty about it, whether it is of the devil or of God, and have somewhat hastily concluded that it is the chief end of man here to "glorify God and enjoy him forever."

I was in awe and in love at the same time. My soul would whisper to my mind as my eyes read words that it had never seen before and chanted softly, *You found me, you found me!* My practice was to read a section before breakfast or after lunch, and whisk myself away as if I was walking on air. So light those words made me feel, so free.

That particular time was also appropriate for the intake of knowledge as I was on a six-month "retreat," and isolated from monastery traditions of having evening drinks in the rec room, a separate floor dedicated to enjoying time off with your brother monks informally.

As soon as the two-year process of actually becoming a monk is all said and done, one then enters the retreat period for six months in order to stay separate for a time, study, get used to being on the property after hours, and using your hut for evening meditation and study. Solitude was a foundational marker of every rank promotion in the monastery. Once a promotion to a new rank is approved, there's ceremony followed by solitude. A humbling process meant to take away any potential for pride and ego-enhancement from the new position.

I was finally becoming the philosopher I set out to be. All day I would test my new knowledge with the other monks, and discuss the deepest truths that have plagued man since man developed higher order thinking, all while painting, growing food, building structures, cleaning and landscaping the expansive 51-acre jungle home. I was at peace, especially when reading from the discourses of Plato. I had spent time to read every discourse that caught my attention, and eventually that meant all of them. Consider the following from *The Republic,*

As in learning to read, first we acquire the elements or letters separately, and afterwards their combinations, and cannot recognize reflections of them until we know the letters themselves;—in like manner we must first attain the elements or essential forms of the virtues, and then trace their combinations in life and experience. There is a music of the soul which answers to the harmony of the world; and the fairest object of a musical soul is the fair mind in the fair body. Some defect in the latter may be excused, but not in the former. True love is the daughter of temperance, and temperance is utterly opposed to the madness of bodily pleasure.

By reading Socrates, I was able to fully understand the logic behind my path. I finally understood why so many students lacked appreciation for their university enrolment, and mistake that precious time in their lives for fun instead of growth, and why historians learned what they learned and taught what they taught. The very act of acquiring knowledge made my brain feel massaged and I could not wait for the next page, or the next discourse, or the next great figure in history who would teach me. In the texts and the words, words, words of figures throughout history, I met those who had taken the time to study life and the mind. They explained to me how people made choices as well as why people felt the way they felt. I discovered I had so much to live for, and I knew that I was going to absorb a great deal of information by taking the time to read and learn from the very philosophers I admired and attempted to emulate.

In those years, my knowledge of Hindu ceremony increased along with my understanding and study of Sanskrit. I became a priest for the monastery's temple. I undertook the study of the well-known, Hindu chant Sri Rudram, taking some 30 minutes to chant fully, and I started to perform the early morning simple guru ceremonies that all the monks attended, along with group chanting at the major festivals. As for work, my artisan senior Teja trained me in plumbing, woodwork, light electrical work, landscaping, vehicle maintenance, general construction and repair, and the growing and harvesting of fresh organic food.

Inside the office, I was taught the department's work order programs for monastery maintenance as well as how to take ownership of a work order, which included assessing it and either completing it or reporting back to the group for discussion. The team aspect was new to me, but once I got the hang of being a subordinate, respecting team harmony and communicating better the environment became extremely enjoyable. The more harmonious I was, the better everyone else treated me. I no longer needed an unfounded, innate respect from the group; instead, I worked hard for the little praise or blame I got and was content. I was thriving.

My daily routine was exhausting but effective for my mental health, and I took up physical training in the small monastery gym so my body could handle the work—both in the temple and in the field. As soon as I became eligible for the temple vigils— three-hour shifts taken around the clock—I was considered a real monk. I had already taken vows, wore robes and beads, and I was a monk, but you don't fully join the brotherhood in the eyes of the group until you put in the same work as everyone else, and that meant sleep deprivation training. At that point, I was trained to go without food and simple comforts, but going without sleep would soon prove to be the most difficult task I'd ever undertaken.

If you are able to see the world from a true present moment of ongoing perfection, no problem has ever risen and no problem will ever exist.

Well, what the hell does that mean; of course, there are problems in the world and problems in my life. There is chaos intermingled with order, and everything devastating *and* mundane in between. And that thought is valid, that way of thinking is true, but truth is relative. There are bits of knowledge and experience you think are true today that will no longer be useful next year. The same is true for our day-to-day consciousness. The way you think at this moment will be different from the way you are thinking tomorrow, or the next day, or the day after that. But regardless of how you are thinking, it is, indeed, truth if it creates a solution for you when it is needed on your own timeline, and no one else can take that away.

The concept is to zoom out of your normal consciousness, zoom out far enough so you can see the entire planet at once. You can see all the oceans as one body of water, the continents and countries as the same land without borders, and beyond that is outer space, beyond that the galaxy, and beyond that the universe, and we don't really know what goes on beyond that. We can use this type of awareness shifting to detach and see our small lives a little more clearly. Not everything is as important as you think it is because you are too close to it. But when we expand our awareness far back enough, we can begin to see that everything is happening in a systematic and complete way. It takes a little faith, takes a lot of meditation, and it takes practice, but eventually you can bring your awareness to the present moment, every moment, all the time.

A modern, present individual is not living in the past or the future. True modern thought is uncomplicated and right now.

Modern living as a modern person is living in the now, being completely current and without stress, even in the midst of activity and pressure-driven results.

One of the training tools I use with clients is to get into this thought strata, to understand all action is inevitable, and you, as an actor, are just a witness observing it all around you. Enjoy, don't rush or feel pushed. Just act, breathe, and know that everything that happens is good and meant to be.

* * *

I was given the 3-6am Ganesha (elephant-faced deity) vigil for my first year of temple shifts. I woke up at 2am, walked in from my hut and picked flowers along the way. The rule was to shower at least 30 minutes before your shift but most showered right before so they were bright and fresh for their temple duties. I would get my flowers, shower up and make espresso before entering the back door where the priests entered. A dark, narrow hallway led you around to the side of the main shrine where Siva Nataraja stood.

The Siva deity was something to behold. Standing about five feet and on top of a three-foot tiled base, the statue towered over me and demanded attention. Not to mention, the deity was made of a metal alloy; so, after a good polishing with lemons and Vibhuti powder, her golden skin would glow.

Every third hour the priest on duty would begin to ring the bells at each of the three shrines, indicating that there was a temple shift taking place. If the next monk to take the shift was more than one minute late, he would have to perform another three-hour shift in 24 hours. If he was more than 30 minutes late, he could not do the current shift and the priest currently on duty was to remain in the temple for an additional three-hour shift. The penalty falls on both the monk in the temple and the one who was late, making him realize that his duties, when left incomplete or abandoned, affected others not just him.

The 3am shift was one of the easiest to accomplish. As monks, we already had to wake up early, and the 3am temple duty gave one a head start to a strong day. There was no sympathy for exhaustion when on most of the temple vigils. If one was more tired than usual he was left alone to figure out how to get stronger and build more mental toughness. I did the 3am duty for exactly one year and did well; in fact, I flourished. I found no part of it difficult and I even went to all of the early morning meditations even though the 9pm, 12 and 3am were exempt. The difficulty did not begin until I began the most challenging temple shift there was, The Midnight.

The Midnight, as it is known, was the 12 to 3am temple shift held every day for at least one month. I was given the midnight shift indefinitely for my first assignment after performing a year of the 3am shift. I didn't know when it would end, nor did I care. The respect and gratitude for performing The Midnight was obvious amongst the brothers, and it showed in their greetings each day. The Midnight Monk, or Viligee as we were referred to, was allowed to be exhausted and confused due to their extreme discipline. The monk on the midnight shift had to be up by 11:30pm, in the temple by 11:59 and ready to perform their three-hour temple duties with vigor. They were allowed to sleep after the shift around 3:15am, once they made the walk to their hut, and were to be at work for their 8am morning meeting, showered, fed and ready to go.

For me, it was different. I wanted to stand out even more; I wanted to be the best. Instead of taking the normal sleeping privileges and getting up groggy and sluggish for the 8am meeting, I woke at 6:45am and downed a protein shake I'd made a few hours earlier. I then walked to the gym and began lifting weights until I had to get ready for work. I ended up going to bed around 9pm, up at 11pm and asleep again from 3:30 to 6:45am. That's roughly five hours broken up into two naps. I did The

Midnight discipline for nine months straight, and it nearly drove me insane. The first six months went well and I thrived on the intense discipline. But the last three months of sleep deprivation were giving me hallucinations throughout the day. I was also unable to understand basic conversation or follow directions. After a while, I became numb to the exhaustion and entered into the famous "zombie" state that monks could see from across the room.

One of the interesting lifestyle aspects about being a monk is the forced discipline. Monks don't have spouses or children, and the workplace is not extremely stressful as you're surrounded by calm monks. What the discipline is allowing is a door into another world, a world where calmness, stress and carefree living go away and the individual is tested on their ability to survive under circumstances of hardship. Then, when a monk has seen his body and mind reach the lowest depths of misery, he is brought back up into the world of the living. Each and every monk is metaphorically taken by the skin of their neck, dipped into a vat of boiling water, and pulled back out to dry, rest and recover. When the ordeal is over, he is to be that much stronger, that much more willing to endure everything else — especially the mundane.

It is the mundane that truly tests our willpower. The day-to-day experience ends up being the greatest test of will that a human can endure. Once we capture joy in our normal everyday life, we have uncovered the mystery that surrounds our existence. It is the small daily moments that comprise our life, and to conquer the moment is to conquer all of life. Seeing the joy in the simple, the regular aspects of life that we normally take for granted — like water — become the ultimate experience. The mountains are still mountains after our transformation but we see them as the truly miraculous structures they are. We begin to see all of life for what it is — a miracle.

Do not mistake the practice of meditation for the goal.

Many people feel they need to meditate every day. They are under the impression that when meditation is happening, there is a reaction of mind and body that will not be present after meditating — and this is true to a degree. However, after a while, the meditator should become anchored in the goal and not anchored in the practice.

The goal of meditation comes in many forms based off of one's understanding of what meditation does, or what a human is even capable of. Some need to calm down, lower their blood pressure, reduce anxiety, achieve some form of homeostasis and restore mental health. Others wish to achieve a form, or lack thereof, of transcendence. Leaving the body and mind behind for a while, and unlocking an omniscient form of peace, is something a rare few will seek, and an even smaller number of people will reach.

Whatever the goal, the aphorism remains the same. If your practice is not creating a new being and a new ability to remain at peace when the meditation is over, then the practice lacks depth. Eventually, an accomplished meditator using a well-structured system only needs to "touch in" from time to time, at most four or five days a week for 20 to 30 minutes a session. The rest of the time can be spent on other tasks that benefit the individual, and the individual's family or circle of influence.

* * *

After serving nine long months on The Midnight, I was taken off by the direction of my seniors. It's possible that I could have gone longer, but my health began to deteriorate and I could no longer work as effectively as before. However, the results were a success. In the eyes of the elders and fellow brothers, I had passed the challenge by never once asking for a break, nor did I want one. I was fully ready to become ill for what I believed in, and had to some degree.

The shift was split between another monk, sharing the burden with a month on/month off schedule. I had January/March/May/July, etc, and he had the in-between months. Oddly enough, that was also a difficult transition. Once one was just getting into the groove of sleep deprivation, it was over and full rest was available again. But that's exactly when insomnia would set in and the body was ready to stay up all night. When the insomnia subsided and the body got used to being off the discipline, it was time to go back into the trenches for a new month. And so the cycle continued for the rest of my monastic life. I was one of the few monks who never complained, so they had no choice but to keep me on the midnight duty.

Occasionally, I would commiserate with an older monk who performed the midnight shift for 15 years. I sought his advice and received counsel on how to continue, and basically would just cry on his shoulder for a few minutes. He even ended up requesting a new shift after those 15 long years, and his request was granted after six months of negotiations.

My memory isn't clear on the matter, but after some time The Midnight took its toll on me. After about nine years of that exhausting sleep schedule, my inner-vision about what I was doing became distorted. I'd look around at everyone who slept well and wonder if I was being used for my naive strength. I would notice those who never had this challenging discipline and question if there wasn't a suspicious purpose to it. After a while, I became bitter and more aloof from the group, considering myself much stronger than the others, and no longer relating to those who had never seen years of sleep deprivation training.

My delusions brought me into a state of mental loneliness, and I made my schedule even more rigorous and trained in our gym three times a day—sometimes beginning the first session at 3am. Getting so deeply involved in my own pursuits led me to getting a budget to finish building the monastery's first gym. When I became a monk, there were only tents put up for exercise; then, later, trailers carved into, and eventually, I found a permanent gym home on the ground floor of a house, seated on 19 acres of land acquired by the monks. No one used the ground floor except for some old equipment storage, and there was only gravel as a floor and cobwebs for walls. I began working out on the gravel and would bring the treadmill over from the exercise trailer to use for cardio on rainy days. I found scrap lumber and put it down for flooring, and even grabbed carpet from a renovation being done at the main building and used it for a designated yoga and gymnastics area. Soon enough, the place looked in decent shape and my energy was being put into it. Monks would walk by and see the operation developing. Some would give thanks for providing a space for everyone to use, while others would watch and think I was causing trouble by making my own space and going around the seniors—a practice frowned upon in the organization.

> The revolutionary hero re-orders the protective structure of society, when the emergence of an anomaly makes such re-ordering necessary. He is therefore the agent of change, upon whose actions all stability is predicated. This capacity—which should make him a welcome figure in every community—is exceedingly threatening to those completely encapsulated by the status quo, and who are unable or unwilling to see where the present state of adaptation is incomplete, and where residual danger lies. The archetypal revolutionary hero therefore faces the anger and rejection of his peers, as well as the terrors of the absolutely unknown.
> Dr. Jordan B. Peterson

The monastery was, indeed, a powerful place, but it also had some very strange aspects. What I began to notice was a culture of dysfunction. We were to live in a confined compound for a long time, and for many of the monks, this pressure resulted in an obsession over small details and watching over everything. It would get worse the less those monks had to do to preoccupy their time. They would worry about what others were doing, mentally obsessing over others' actions, and living inside their brother's life, rather than their own. I started to stand out as an individual, pushing beyond the boundaries of what most monks would do, and that was not a good idea for the longevity of my monastic rank.

The same situation exists for people out in the world, the workplace especially. We get comfortable in our routine and eventually stop growing. The next challenge then becomes bringing other people down so you remain on an elevated level. Other people who push back against the system of order and bring chaos, individuality, and novelty, will start to make those who thrive in comfort and order uneasy. Their system has existed for so long it cannot possibly stand the test of novelty as it could bring a theory, philosophy or history crashing down. It wasn't that I planned all of this out, it's just that my nature couldn't allow me to do the same thing for too long without making it better or improving the situation somehow. It's also not true that the monastery is against change, but too much too soon was considered risky. The normal pace of a project in the monastery would take years to accomplish. However, when I see something in my mind I try to produce it in the physical world quickly, or get the ball rolling right away so the energy is there to meet the challenge of moving the forces of the physical world. Instead of asking, I would just do, and that eventually led to my downfall as a monk and my success as a mentor and coach in the world.

Meanwhile, the leadership tactics in my department were wearing on me. I would misunderstand orders and was, consequently, gaslighted and made to feel like I was crazy and in the wrong. I would be told one thing by my senior in private, and told another thing by the same senior in a group of people. I tried to lead as best I could, but didn't actually have any say whatsoever. In my opinion, when a team is built on a foundation of implicit harmony and perfection—they can do no wrong or else—unhealthy amounts of expectation build within the group. This "safe space" environment eventually crumbles as each member of the team is exposed as being a normal human with feelings, weaknesses, and desires. When natural arguments and disagreements do arise, the ones involved are deemed unfit for the job and criticized for not keeping with the incredibly high standards.

I couldn't actually criticize anyone's work because we were all "equal," and I had little freedom in areas of growth. The constrained environment made it difficult to expand my knowledge due to the group's dependence on the leader. I could not justify the means for the ends after long.

Energy remains energy, regardless the conduit.

The energy you manifest expresses itself in myriad forms. Sometimes that's anger, love, frustration or joy; whatever the expression, the force essence remains the same.

You are a driving force of energy. Just as electricity expresses itself through computers yet remains electricity all the same, your emotions are driven by an energy that remains itself at its core. Frustration, anger, love, lust, power, weakness, whatever the emotion or action: it is all driven by a pure energy that doesn't change.

We want to harness that energy and express it through the channel we want. If we don't, it comes out at random, basing its movement by the actions of other people, situations or society; you become a puppet on a string. The steps to harness that force are as follows: attention, concentration, meditation, contemplation. Once the steps are sustained in a practical and consistent routine, you will harness your own energy naturally.

Attention begins with the process of self-observation and detachment. Self-observation is also called mindfulness. We slowly become aware of ourselves from an outside perspective and can see ourselves and everyone else at the same time. This leads to an introspective lifestyle that forces you to eventually see the world from the inside out, instead of the outside in.

* * *

I will always be grateful for the training I went through in the SK and grateful for my mentor and artisan, and I do wish I could have been a better apprentice. But in the end, after seven years of training, I quit my job and decided I wouldn't work for the SK any longer. One morning I grabbed my things out of my desk, packed it all up in a box, and sent in my letter of resignation.

This was a difficult and risky decision that no monk had ever actually done before. I was potentially risking being kicked out of the monastery for disobedience, but it was worth it.

The events leading up to the decision had driven me over the edge as I'd experienced enough of the dualistic leadership tactics used by my department and I was ready to move on. It was no mystery that my department head was a slave driver, and he was known for his extremely high standards, but over the years his three-hour long rants and lectures on how poor we performed didn't sit right with me and I fought back. I was being groomed to one day take over the position of department head, but it wasn't worth being emotionally discouraged and psychologically beaten down. That is one part of the job I couldn't do and it went against all my morals on how to lead a team of people, people that you want to be better than you, more capable and empowered. This was the opposite. I felt worse after each performance evaluation and no other department head cared to do anything about it, even my guru.

One afternoon in 2014, after having served in the department for seven years, I turned in my letter of resignation to my team leader. I packed up my things in a box and left it there for the weekend. I had enough and it was time to let everyone know that something needed to change. Earlier that afternoon, I made my schedule as the boss requested and I reported it to him. After seeing he was displeased and hearing him begin to speak, something inside me gave way. I could feel the hair on my neck raise, my cheeks filled with heat and my heart started to explode out of my chest. I argued that I couldn't possibly achieve the amount of work he expected and still keep the quality and high standard at the same time.

In a three-hour period, I was in charge of managing the organic garden's work schedule for the week, and complete several difficult tasks in the office for the database. Along with that were maintenance jobs that needed my attention, all with detailed notes now required of how long each task took and why—within a small window that almost seemed designed to make you fail.

After performing better and better every year and getting nothing in return, I snapped and said no. My usual carefree demeanor turned harsh and I decided that I wouldn't be fit to stay under the command of an unfit leader who didn't take any criticism from a subordinate. I lost my cool and raised my voice and demanded more respect and appreciation for the amount of success I had in making an impact in several key aspects of the department. What ensued was another three-hour lecture on how we were the least accomplished department and how no one respected our group as a whole. I fumed inside whilst sitting quietly, listening to someone I respect and admire tell me I would never be good enough if I continued to be the person I was—and I liked the person I was. I knew at that moment that my seven-year training was over and I was leaving the department no matter the cost.

Senior leadership received word of my decision and held a meeting with all of the team leaders. I was given an immediate order to not do any work for any department until further notice and to take leave of normal monastic duties for three days. My guru told me to "go within and spend time in nature." I did as he asked and spent the next three days as an outsider, spending my time on the outskirts of the grounds, sweeping the temple, walking the woods and meditating on my decision. I didn't attend the group ceremonies, nor did I go to lunch or dinner. I made sure not to be seen for those days and not disturb the work going on in other areas.

One young monk who took vows at the same time I did, Nandi, helped support me in quiet. He would walk out to where I was and spend an hour talking, and he would catch me up to the rumblings going on at the main building. No one was quite sure what to do since a monk had never renounced his department before. I was sure it was over for me, and I was okay with that. I was ready to stand up for what I believed in, and I was hedging my bet that the monastery needed me for the value I provided.

The seniors decided I would talk with the Acharyas, or senior circle of monks, on an individual basis to hear my side of the story and explain my intentions. Over the next few days I sought them out and had long discussions, repeating my side of the story and what was going on in my head. No doubt the sleep deprivation helped form my inability to absorb the same pressures of the department, but at the same time I was convinced that I was morally and ethically right.

After several days the elders decided in my favor, and I was sent to the media department to begin training with an older group of monks who were more relaxed and experienced in working with independent, "maverick"-type individuals. It was there that I learned to professionally write, proofread, edit and publish works. I helped manage up to 16 pages of the monastery's international magazine *Hinduism Today*. I coordinated international travel-study programs with 60 participants as well as clerical and assistant duties. I was also responsible for back-end web and blog work. The change of pace was much needed. Over time, I learned that even though I got what I wanted I still hurt someone along the way. Having to burn bridges on the path to crossing them is a painful way to go about life, so be careful. If we burn too many bridges along the way to our goal then we will end up alone without any way out.

If I had a choice to do it all over again, would I choose the same course of action? Yes and no. There are more sensitive ways to get your point across and seek out a solution. I could have spoken with the elders in private as a type of human resources issue, or I could have waited a week for the emotion to fade before approaching my department head. Instead, I chose to abruptly make a change that was sudden, harsh, and cold. In a way that's how I've always been. When I see something in sight that I want, I go after it; I get it and I think and reflect on it later. Ironically enough, that is the very process of success in meditation. If we spend too much time going over the details we will get lost in a cluster of thoughts. The path to enlightenment needs to be led with a sharp sword in order to slice through the forest of thoughts, distractions and side-paths of the mind. We must approach it relentlessly as if the world were ending, at the same time giving patience and trust to the process.

The essence of energy management is self-respect.

We are made up of an everlasting energy that defines how we move, speak, listen and feel, but people are not aware of their ability to tap into this unending well. Understanding our energy and learning how to manage it is understanding our life, mind, and being. Let me make this wide-ranging topic easy for you to learn with four elements that will give you the upper hand at life, love, and the pursuit of happiness.

Element 1: The Energy Equation
There's a clear link between energy and our awareness. Where our awareness goes our energy flows. Instagram, e-mail, the Kardashians—these aspects of life can be likened to strings that pull us this way and that. The reason why we care is because the subject of focus gets our attention whether it deserves it or not.

The equation looks like this:

Our senses (eyes, ears, nose, etc) + Awareness (focus) = energy

Our focus should go to our well-being, the well-being of those we love, those we need to work with or benefit our future in some way. The challenge of energy management system comes when we start to focus on things out of habit, boredom or lack of discipline. Even our thoughts can be as exhausting and unwarranted as toxic people or relationships if left undefined and excessively random.

Element 2: Energy Expenditure
Using energy is inevitable—that's how we stay alive—but what we don't know is that the bulk of our energy goes out of us without us knowing. However, if our energy was like

money we'd keep a watchful eye on the automatic payments of thoughts, relationships and the spoken word—all things that deplete energy.

Most people aren't aware that the smallest things in life take their energy without giving anything back; exhaustion is the result. Giving out energy should be an investment with a good ROI, return on investment. The bigger the energy expenditure, like relationships, the bigger the return should be. Failing relationships are a good example of energy depletion from one partner giving everything and the other not giving nearly enough for a balance.

Make sure that when you give out energy to people, situations or things, they have the ability to give some back. When we get value from something our energy is reciprocated and the energy bank account doesn't get depleted. Giving our energy out and getting nothing in return is not sustainable and will eventually leave us feeling used, bitter, and resentful.

Element 3: Practical Application

We can change our perspective all we want but if we don't start practicing energy management we will never be the effective, powerful, and spontaneously creative person we are meant to be. Use the three Ds to get a firm practice started.

Discrimination + Detachment + Dispassion = Energy Management

Discrimination: We have to consciously be in control of what we give our attention or awareness to. Cultivate observation so that we are aware of things and people around us but are not overly invested. Make sure you develop a personal rule: if you're getting involved then the matter had better be important enough to involve you. If not then detach.

Detachment: The ability to release awareness and thus energy from an object, situation or person. If we observed a situation, person or thing that doesn't need our focus then we let it go, watch from afar and hope everything goes well for those involved. Not everything or everyone should deserve your attention because you value your attention, time and focus. If you don't treat your time and focus as worthy, then everyone and everything will try to take it, use it, and give nothing back. Be the kind of person that makes someone hesitate before involving for fear of wasting your time. Then you have ample energy to give to the things that matter to you, change your life and benefit whoever is involved.

Dispassion: The combination of discrimination and detachment well performed. Our dispassion is a state of wisdom where life bends and wraps around our needs or aversions. If we don't need it then it goes away. If we need it, then the universe presents the door for us to open. Dispassion is being one with our universe and allows the law of attraction to attract that which we need in order to succeed mentally, physically, and spiritually.

Element 4: Cultivating Willpower

The art of a focused meditation system allows us to detach from that which we are aware of, pull all the strings of energy back into our source, and become whole again. With this system we can begin to understand the layers of the mind by actually going through them consciously and choosing how we direct our focus. Meditation is the practice of directing energy, using willpower and getting used to observing life without acting.

Eventually we become a better observer, become more mindful and see life more clearly in the moment. We will be able to catch ourselves when giving too much energy without proper reciprocation and pull back.

* * *

As the years went by I kept to myself, gained more experience, researched history, religious theory, philosophical thought and logic studies. I read many more books covering new aspects related to the mind with psychology, and aspects regarding human belief origins with ancient mythology. The new office position I was in allowed me more access to developing my mind and intellect in a way I never had before. I continued to read the great works of great authors, and I realized I was no longer aspiring to be a philosopher—I had become one. I could use my new writing, speaking and thinking skills to delve into complex subjects and try to understand them as if they were my own teachings. Soon I was online and writing to anyone who would read. I produced short articles that eventually caught the attention of 500 young men who needed a role model, and someone who could teach them what their father failed to.

The work of mentoring so many people became exhausting, so I compiled a manual of all my articles and writings called *A Manual of Success*. The manual was my replacement and a guide for any future young man needing assistance in responsibility, discipline and leadership—for growing up and becoming a man. After months of time off and getting back to my own work, I realized that I had become a much better person by helping others. The trust I gained in those young men had led to increased responsibility and enriched my personal life greatly. I felt a little empty and lost when I took my leave from mentoring, and I didn't know where to direct my energy.

The time away allowed for me to continue writing, and write I did. I wrote two more manuals for the boys to read and learn from, and then I compiled all three manuals into one book and called it *Man in the Making*. Once I released it to the group, I stepped back again and just worked with the few who reached out for questions and deeper insight into my work. Now that I'm out in the world I've actually reconnected with a few of those young men and keep up with their lives and how they are continuing to develop. I felt good about releasing the book to them and I was finally freed to return back to my normal monastic life, helping mentor and guide those who belonged to the church and the monastery's daily visitors—which, as a monk, was considered the main priority.

More years came and went. I traveled and helped with coordination of flights, hotels, entertainment on lavish trips to other islands. I met important people and learned how to act civilized. Life couldn't be better. I was content, challenged and evolving. Meanwhile, my meditation skills were deepening and I was evolving into a new person yet again, a new being that only knew light, love, and upliftment. Meditation is interesting in that way. The more one practices, the more change one sees, much like a caterpillar turning into a butterfly. As I watched myself transition, I started to get interested in other things that weren't really typical for monks. Mountain biking, training in the gym every day, and increasing my overall athletic and intellectual abilities started to take hold and create more interest and passion than my monastic department work. It didn't take long before I was planning the next weekend outing to the bike trails and thinking about it all week.

Liberation comes when you realize all is ego.

I want to end the book with a discussion on ego, perhaps the most misunderstood concept of Eastern mystic thought. The ego acts as our true identity and pretends to be the face of our lives. We are conditioned to agree, living in slavery until our inevitable ego-death. After the dark night is over, the Yogi learns and fully knows he is spirit, eternal, unending and perfect. Ego is not something small nor is it hardly seen or heard; it is big and it has a major impact on our lives. The normal definition of ego according to Google is,

> a person's sense of self-esteem or self-importance.

Google goes on and explains two more definitions that take the concept a little deeper,

> The part of the mind that mediates between the conscious and the unconscious and is responsible for reality testing and a sense of personal identity.

> A conscious thinking subject.

Ego is not just those things but all things. Ego is the very fabric of reality by which we experience our lives and the mask that appears before us as us. It isn't just a "part of the mind" but the whole mind itself. Saying "personal identity" is also correct, but lacking in depth since that definition makes the word exclusive to the "personal" identification. Ego is all that ever was and all that will be. Ego is the hunter, the animal being hunted and the hunt itself. That is the broadest definition possible and the most accurate.

If ego is everything and we are inside of it, then what good does this knowledge have, and how does it apply to us? It applies because ego never makes itself known yet pretends to be in charge of you, me and everyone. Ego tries to control emotions, feelings, whims, fantasies and desires, all the while not being the ultimate identity. There is something greater.

The knowing that everything is ego gives us the upper hand in dealing with the external and internal aspects of the mind. In other words, knowing everything is ego means we can rightfully see and know that which surrounds us and is inside of us, giving us the ability to conquer it. The same idea about ego knowledge applies to everything this book stands for. Everything is your fault means once we know, we can choose; once we choose, we can change. Knowing that the world—and everyone in it—is ego, we can take effective measures to conquer that which displeases us, or that which causes an inordinate amount of suffering.

Seeing our reality as it is—as ego—allows us the freedom to change it because the ego is a tool and not actually in charge. Ego is powerful but not beyond our reach. We can control the ego, we can control ourselves and our reactional, emotional and intellectual behavior. Rising above ego requires a painful process known as the death of the ego. While there is no actual death of ego (as that would imply we were dead) there is a role switch as we take over our rightful place in our lives. The entire process is known as the dark night of the soul.

A creative illness succeeds a period of intense preoccupation with an idea and search for a certain truth. It is a polymorphous condition that can take the shape of depression, neurosis, psychosomatic ailments, or even psychosis. Whatever the symptoms, they are felt as painful, if not agonizing, by the subject, with alternating periods of alleviation and worsening. Throughout the illness the subject never loses the thread of his dominating preoccupation. It is often compatible with normal, professional activity and family life. But even if he keeps to his social activities, he is almost entirely absorbed with himself. He suffers from feelings of utter isolation, even when he has a mentor who guides him through the ordeal (like the shaman apprentice with his master). The termination is often rapid and marked by a phase of exhilaration. The subject emerges from his ordeal with a permanent transformation in his personality and the conviction that he has discovered a great truth or a new spiritual world.

Henri Ellenberger

* * *

I was getting involved in weekend adventures outside the monastery around the time of my Yogi promotion. The rank of Yogi meant I would wear yellow robes and receive larger beads to wear around my neck as well as increase my meditation disciplines and go on a two-year retreat from any news or media going on beyond the monastery walls. The two-year period was known as Yogi *Tapas* or "inner fire." No movies, no news, no talk about anything other than the path of yoga for two years, and also no communicating with family. I began my tapas period a week before President Donald Trump was elected into office, so you can imagine all of the conversations I missed out on.

Before the first day of my two-year discipline, I was allowed to visit family in Texas for four days. I hadn't seen family since I became a monk; they visited shortly after I took vows almost eight years prior, so the trip was important for me. I met my then seven-year-old niece and two-year-old nephew for the first time, which was quite the experience. For a few days I got to be uncle Raj, take my niece around to parks, buy her stuff and share stories. I met my brother-in-law Randy as well, and it was like meeting a brother I never had. Randy gave me a big hug and reassured me that he was taking good care of my sister and looking after the family. I was impressed and relieved at the same time. Just the siblings and kids went out for dinner on one night, and on the last night the whole family got together and I was able to pay for dinner for the first time—that felt good. I made bread for my mom and sisters and made sure to spend one night at each house so no one got jealous.

The last time I had any experience with family was when I was living in the world as a 19-year-old broken man, so the homecoming was able to show me that family is important and they will always be in your life in some manner. Going back to the monastery after the trip was extremely difficult. I kept seeing my niece's face in my head and in my meditations, and I kept thinking about how I would never be able to be there for her as she lived her life. I thought about all the times I'd never be able to go on vacation with my sister's family, and how her husband, Randy, and I had really connected in just four days. I had to put all of that behind me in order to survive the next two years of discipline, and I did; but, who I became over the next two years is someone I never could have imagined.

Upon return to the monastery I took my oath that would last for the next two years. I received my new robes and chopped down my own bamboo staff from our bamboo forest along the outer edges of the property. The straight and strong bamboo staff represented the unwieldy nature of the path and was a stronghold to keep the Yogi grounded and stable. I was to walk with the staff, my heavy beads and new robes until the next rank of Sannyasin presented itself, no shorter than four years. The day I became a Yogi rank I vowed internally to myself to be the best Yogi there was. I vowed to reach a level of mastery that I'd never reached before, go through hardships that burned me from the inside out and become a warrior monk.

Along with reading the works of great authors, autobiography and war history, the two-year period opened up a doorway into the unknown for me. I began to enter what is known as the dark night of the soul where one is subject to the terrors of their own ego's demise, which feels like psychosis. The challenging aspect of this type of depression and aloneness is that it comes from nothing and appears spontaneously, then leaving as mysteriously as it appeared. Months of silence, anger, coldness, depression and questioning came to me and attempted to teach a lesson to my mind. The ego cries as it diminishes and ego is one of the strongest elements of life—it is the fabric of life itself. Losing ego is like losing identity.

During the last year of my monastic life I read two influential books that changed the course of my path and forced me to reevaluate my situation—*Musashi* by Eiji Yoshikawa and *Maps of Meaning: The Architecture of Belief* by Dr. Jordan B. Peterson.

Musashi loosely covers the life of Japanese samurai Miyamoto Musashi, and it carried me through my depression from the dark night of the soul experience. The cold warrior nature of *Musashi* was like a song to my spirit and it kept me from slipping into a state of unresponsiveness altogether. While I wasn't speaking, I was going to work, training in the gym and keeping up with appearances as death slowly took over my being. I would describe the ongoing pain like a fire that persists inside one's body, slowly turning organs, muscles and bones to ash. What doesn't make logical sense is how it all happened and how it all went away.

I was walking in a field after a training session at the gym one afternoon. The weather was calm and uneventful. As usual, I had feelings of being alone, lost, hollow, and near whatever death must feel like, until a mirrored version of myself appeared in front of me. The apparition of myself spoke clearly to me after stopping me in my steps, "I am your worst enemy." The faint phantom burst into flames and blew away in the trade winds. The wall of darkness that had ensconced me for months was gone. I continued walking but now I was new, born again and fresh. Sadness turned to contentment, fog turned to clarity, madness turned to intelligence. The monastery that had welcomed a young man 12 years prior was now housing an entirely different man. I looked the same on the outside but on the inside I was new, and I could see life from the perspective of freedom. It was as if I was playing a game and in control of my actions, my reactions, my thoughts, my expressions and my character.

The crushing effects of ego death are sad, scary and slow. One can never know where or when it is going to happen, or how it breeds a new soul inside the same body. How could it steal me away from myself and replace me with something entirely new? I could now look in the mirror and know who I was, where I was going and what my future held. The very truths that were deeply ingrained in me were gone and I saw life for what it was; I saw the mind for what it was; and I saw people for who they were.

The deconstruction of ego and the resurrection of Self is a painfully liberating process that cannot be avoided if Self-realization is to be achieved. One may have the internal success at meditation, but must eventually reap the rewards on the outside and experience the dark night of the soul. What happened to me was the result of years of hard work. Transformation is not sudden when involving the mind and spirit. It's as if I had been a string that began to burn at one end when I stepped into the monastery, and finally had burned through to the other side, revealing the inner truth that had been there all along.

Other initiations involve a descent to the realm of the dead; for example, the future medicine man goes to sleep by the burying ground, or enters a cave, or is transported underground or to the bottom of a lake. Among some tribes, the initiation also includes the novice's being "roasted" in or at a fire. Finally, the candidate is resuscitated by the same Supernatural Beings who had killed him, and he is now "a man of Power." During and after his initiation he meets with spirits, Heroes of the mythical Times, and souls of the dead—

and in a certain sense they all instruct him in the secrets of the medicine man's profession. Naturally, the training proper is concluded under the direction of the older masters. In short, the candidate becomes a medicine man through a ritual of initiatory death, followed by a resurrection to a new and superhuman condition.

Mircea Eliade

Now that I had a fresh pair of eyes to see new truths again, Jordan B. Peterson's work *Maps of Meaning: The Architecture of Belief* had come into my life. I began to read the exhausting and complex book every day. The book is so hard to read that I had to spend a week on the first chapter, reading the pages again and again to understand the concepts Peterson brings out in his work. In the meantime, my body was inside a monastery and my mind outside the walls and exploring the world. I began a process of being aloof from work and worried more about other aspects of my character that had taken prominence. *Maps of Meaning* began to go alongside my own life as if I was reading about my current predicament. Group identity of monastic life had run its course and I sought to spread my newfound wings and fly out into the world from whence I'd come.

The final page of Peterson's book echoed the life I was now trying to understand, deconstruct, and validate. I now needed something to convince me—either stay on as a monk and never change, or go out into the world in order to face the mythological dragon of chaos once again. The dragon is the unknown, unexplored and potentially fatal reality. The unpredictable nature of the mythological dragon of chaos is what drives humans either to succeed, or to fail miserably.

The dragon limits the pursuit of individual interest. The struggle with the dragon—against the forces that devour will and hope—constitutes the heroic battle, in the mythological world. Faithful adherence to the reality of personal experience ensures contact with the dragon—and it is during such contact that the great force of the individual spirit makes itself manifest, if it is allowed to. The hero voluntarily places himself in opposition to the dragon. The liar pretends that the great danger does not exist, to his peril and to that of others, or abdicates his relationship with his essential interest, and abandons all chance at further development.

Over the next several months I deconstructed the work of Dr. Peterson and began to understand his chaos/order theories. The new knowledge and perspective was like a fresh breath of air, something new for me to understand the world with. The Eastern philosophies I'd been learning were enough to understand what I had done up to this point in life, but what I was now facing was what to do for the rest of it.

Upon finishing the book, I knew deep down my fate was to move on and seek out the next challenge, the next dragon of chaos that would force me to change chaos into order and restore peace to the world I appeared from. Just like I had known years before, deep down in the core of my being, that I was to leave the world and become a master of meditation and a monk of the jungle, I now knew it was time to leave the monastery. A new message, a new order had taken hold of my consciousness and I obeyed. It felt good to come to the realization that I was going to leave the monastery eventually and continue my experience elsewhere.

Throughout the changes going on in my mind, I had the guts to reach out for assistance and support. Taking one look at me one could tell I was in bad shape, exhausted and confused, and needed someone to talk to. Monks would approach me casually and ask if everything was alright knowing full well I had just finished a three-month role-playing exercise as a psychopath. Everyone knew about the dark night of the soul and was cautious to try and help. A few close monks would walk with me or sit and have tea, telling me all about their dark night and the terrible onslaught of spiritual progress. They were so sweet to give me their time and explain things that they had told no one else. You find out all kinds of things you didn't know about someone else in times of desperation; we find out that we all actually go through similar experiences and are all the same in our pains and burdens.

One monk would tell me of his time with his guru, having things he loved taken away and being tested in order to be a better monk. Others would tell me of the times they visited home and had a difficult time coming back to monastic life. The one theme that held every story together is that they all made it through the dark night and remained as monks. But I looked around and began to see people that were held up and kept together by a shared story, a myth that this all made sense in some mysterious way. I, on the other hand, wasn't convinced. I knew that this didn't have to be the case and I could live a good life in the outside world. Why have things stripped away from me in order to be tested? Why can't spiritual life also include people you love and care about?

I was in the brewery when the sudden realization occurred, "I am done here," came to mind. For some reason I grabbed my phone and texted my eldest sister Rose, the one who had trained me to live on the island so many years earlier, "Rose, I'm ready to come home now. I don't want to be a monk anymore."

I felt like a child for some reason. As if I'd been at a friend's house for 12 years and now I was ready to leave and go back to life again. It felt very strange but also extremely exciting to type those words to my sister. She was ecstatic and called me within minutes. "Do you need to be picked up? We can come get you, oh my god what a relief!" The thought of her actually coming to pick me up as if I was just over in the next town made me smile. I had a few tears falling from my eyes as I let her know that I couldn't leave just yet, but I would get a ticket to wherever I wanted to go once the decision was final. It would take a few days to process out and let everyone know what was going on.

I e-mailed my guru and my department head letting them know I had decided to leave the monastery. The monks were on their weekend schedule so not much was going to happen right away.

The truth is that we can have a wonderful life in whatever pursuit we want. We can be spiritual and loving people right here in the world. I realized then that being a monk isn't about mastering meditation and living as a spiritual being — that was only a by-product, a consequence of the path itself. Being a renunciate monk and living only with other monks is just about sacrificing one's own life for the religion — both for its followers and its upkeep. One becomes a monk in order to focus on selfless service to the devotees, as some sort of middleman with God on one end and the devout and pious on the other. It took me years to make sense of it all but it hit me all at once; I was always living as a monk, thinking that being a monk was only inside monasteries. *Only inside here*, I thought, *could I live this way*, but it isn't true at all.

I never signed up to renounce my life for Hinduism, and I certainly didn't do it for the devotees. I became a monk in order to do two things. First, I wanted to master meditation. I needed to understand my mind and go through the trials of resolving my past in order to have a crystal clear vision of how to navigate inside meditation and come out the other end. I did that. I did the work and learned the system so well that I was meditating in deep states of consciousness with ease. Second, I wanted to experience discipline and hardship in the form of psychological duress and pain. I wanted to experience what the path of yogic training was all about, the ins and outs of renouncing the world and turning my back on it. I did that. I went through the no eating and sleeping disciplines. I went through the no bed, no comforts and only wearing rags phase of my life. I left the world and conquered my greatest fear—my fear of being homeless. And, it was my guru who reminded me of everything I came there for.

After I wrote to him about my intention to leave, my guru and I had a meeting in his office the next day. He asked me what he could do for me. I explained I was ready to move on and he asked where I would like to go—it was all very simple, until I burst into tears. Bodhinatha, my guru, calmed me down and pulled out a sheet of paper with my handwriting on it. Twelve years prior to this day I was asked to write out an explanation as to why I was becoming a monk. My first two sentences explained it all: I wanted to master meditation and experience "tapas" or the inner fire of spiritual progress and discipline. He showed me what I wrote and then explained that everything was perfect, I had done what I came there to do and was now ready to move on—and he couldn't be happier with my decision. My guru knew all along that I had been struggling the past few months, and he knew it was because my time had come. Just like my nervous system broke down as a young monk and my former self had collided with the new, now my current self was going through the pain of meeting its newer version. The pain I had felt, the pain everyone feels in spiritual progress throughout life, is the merging of one reality against another. This friction of two beings and two paths becoming one creates heat which is experienced as struggle and pain. Going from one way of living to another, one way of thinking to another, and going from one version of yourself to another takes time for it all to work. The nervous system experiences it first in the form of depression and confusion, then the mind starts to see what's going on as the body flows into the transition, making it complete. Finally, the area that surrounds you is different and the transition has taken place.

I felt better. I felt relieved by my guru's support and guidance as always. I never left his office confused or upset. I decided to get a ticket to Austin, Texas, to stay with the majority of my family, and visit my father in Chicago after settling into the world. After that meeting, I had the next 48 hours to pack, settle all of my work by passing it on to another monk, say my goodbyes, turn in my computer, phone, and robes, and then leave. Bodhinatha gave me one last mission in Texas, which I fulfilled a few days after landing, and said to me, "Don't forget what you learned."

I had two meetings with my former department head. It had been about four years since the two of us had met together, the last formal meeting being an explanation as to why I quit his department. These last two meetings with him, one on the first day of transitioning and right before I left for the airport, were the sweetest of times I experienced in his office. We fully resolved our issues and he explained some things I would experience out here in the world. I felt so light after we talked and I knew that he still had love and appreciation for me.

One of the most challenging meetings I had was with my current department head. He made sure that I understood how bad of an idea it was to leave and enter the "cruel" world. That was the saddest meeting for me as I always respected him and thought so highly of his maturity; but, when he found out I was leaving, he tried to scare me with guilt tactics and I saw the real man behind the beard.

I talked with one of the oldest monks there for about an hour before my ride came to take me to the airport. He was so very sweet and kind, and gave me some amazing advice as to the astrology and mysticism of my decision, and the impact it had on other, more subtle, worlds.

I cried with a senior monk brother of mine who wished me well and knew that I would do great things and help many people. This monk, Teja, was the first to train me in the field. For seven years he helped support my evolution, by helping me go from a young and dumb know-it-all to a respectable laborer with many skills. He taught me not only the skills listed in the beginning of this book, but most importantly he showed me what a true devotee and monk looks like. Teja not only taught the practical nature of work, but he was the living example. He could embrace the suck of challenges and hardship with a smile, take orders and give them out in a kind and harmonious way. Teja was always a well-respected monk and everyone knew his work ethic was far beyond what anyone asked for. He was the first to show up and the last to leave at the end of the day, worked the hardest in the gym and was soft spoken and admired by his seniors. I'll never forget Teja and the amazing seven years with him.

The young monks Jayanatha, Mayuranatha and Dayanatha all said their goodbyes. These young fellows all came after me and I got the chance to see them grow up and become men inside the monastery just like I had in the years prior. It was an honor to hear them wish me well in my new journey.

Some monks didn't want to speak with me, or look at me, and I'm okay with that. I understand why they would feel that way, I understood what they were feeling. Most of our monastic training revolved around being a good soldier-monk, not treating anyone with special attention or becoming friends. Yes, we were brothers, but brothers of an eternal order that stood for knowledge, truth and wisdom. We didn't act like brothers of a family because we weren't, and our training allowed us to explore being alone and aloof from relationships of any intimate nature. There was no "brotherly love" as you would imagine, but there was a respect for each individual for the sacrifice they had taken under vows—and I could see now that the same respect others had for me the day before, still being a monk, was now gone. That respect was for the vow you had chosen, not who you were in essence and in spirit. Most will probably think that philosophy is cold and not intuitive to the monk ideology, and they would be correct most of the time. It is the Unusual and Unique that confuses people, and that's exactly what my training was. We were soldiers first—alone, banded together for the same goal—and happy, contented, loving monks second. There was a reason we were called "soldiers of the within" and not "monks living together in harmony."

I trust you.

Being a philosopher for such a long time has helped me understand the world from another perspective. You would think my work involves a lot of love, appreciation, gratitude and upliftment—but that's actually not the case.

Throughout the week I work with people, both online and in person, that struggle to live another day. I wake up to e-mails from people asking how they are going to get over the loss of their child. In other words, people ask me why they should even wake up anymore. Some people are on the brink of ending it all, and they tell me about it. I've been hired by some people to make sure they survive the week in what seems to be a world of hurt, pain and suffering. And, the interesting part about it all is that I agree.

The world is suffering. More accurately, the world contains suffering. You will suffer; I will go through hardship; we will all be tested as to whether we can sustain living in an unbearable world. Why? Why would we go through this?

As I've talked with people over the last few years about pain and trauma, I've come to learn that we have no choice in the matter. The dragon of chaos is going to approach, the predictable world around us is going to change—and crumble—and the unknown, unpredictable and anomaly-ridden future will present itself like some kind of ritualistic mating call.

The world, and all of its variety, allows the combination of both disaster and promise to occur. No one is controlling it from the sky, there's no great "mystery" to God's will except to experience that which has been thrown together. It's not random though, and that's what allows us to keep going. Deep down we know there is some sense of divinity, of success and some possibility of survival—and even thriving.

There's something inside us that knows right after the chaos, right after the unpredictable comes the world of explored territory. We start to see again, feel better again, sense that the world around us is becoming more manageable—again. This is what keeps us alive because we are all heroes of our own story.

We all share a shared story—we all suffer, have suffered or will suffer again. It's coming, it has come or it is come. We are always each phase of the experiencer, the experience and the experienced. Together we share this common story, myth and tale that keeps us from ending it all. It's the "what if" of our lives. It's the "could be."

I often ask those clients who are not sure if they will make it to tomorrow, to give me five minutes, then 10, then an hour. We slowly open up our vision and can accept a short future before a longer one. Give me a day eventually turns into, "I'll see you next week."

We survive the burden of our existence by making ourselves the explorer of that which surrounds us. We have to face the chaos and the hurt in order to succeed. In order to face the dread and unpredictable nature of tomorrow we have to become brave, courageous, and strong—and then we can see that "tomorrow" wasn't so bad, and "next week" now seems possible.

I've come to learn that our actions create who we are. We play the role of the hero by facing pain courageously, or we face it as broken and shattered individuals and let it eat us alive. Either way, the dragon of chaos remains always engulfing itself, recreating life, exploration and chaos only for us to face it again. Understanding this, we can arm ourselves with knowledge, courage, and bravery. We can face the knowable unknowable and, this time, we can choose to win.

Eventually, we learn that we never did it for ourselves. We went through the pain of suffering, the burden of living, and faced the ever-repeating dragon of consciousness in order to one day look someone in the eyes and say, "Can you make it to tomorrow?"

* * *

My friend and tattoo artist, Jarod Powell, came to pick me up in the front of the monastery gates at the welcome gazebo. Just like I had been dropped off 12 years ago and waited in that very structure, I was waiting for my ride back to life as a civilian. Jarod came early so he could take me out to brunch and have drinks and laughs before catching my flight. He had a big smile on his face as I got in the car. His music was incredibly loud and he had to shout in order to be heard, "Welcome to the world, brother!" I smiled and gave my thanks for his generosity. I learned as we drove off that he too was on the island for 12 years and was making his way to Washington to tattoo with a friend there. His motorcycles were being shipped off island and he asked if I wanted to have my mountain bikes in the same container. I thanked him again and said, "Thanks, but nothing there was mine."

We headed to a breakfast place down the road a bit, but stopped when we saw one of Jarod's friends selling flavored coconut waters. He said I would love his friend's concoctions and that we had to get some. I looked a little closer and noticed I knew the man selling the drinks.

"Hello," I said to the large bearded alchemist. "Do you remember me?"

"Yes. I met you about 12 years ago in the monastery. You're the guy who kicked me out."

When I was a young monk, fresh on the scene and excited to enforce the law in any way I could, I ended up making an enemy of a man who repeatedly came onto the property unannounced and after visiting hours. I was asked to go out with Teja and get him off the property, except I was not very nice about it. The local Hawaiian trespasser actually considered the grounds sacred, but he always came in the back entrance instead of the front. I would yell at him and tell him to get out, that he wasn't welcome. One day he came with a friend, also large and bearded, and my department head asked this time for him to be brought to his office to speak with him. There I was in a Mule, our 4x4 vehicle, asking to take the local trespasser into the office headquarters of my senior. He obliged, hopped in the front seat and was quiet. I told him that I honestly had nothing genuine to say to him, and that I was just following orders. He smiled and said that it was okay, he understood.

My department head towered over the local by a few feet and greeted him with a smile. I stood and watched as if a fight was about to break out, but all that happened was a friendly conversation. It was all probably just to teach me a lesson in working with others, and not for the local at all. After they exchanged pleasantries about where the local lived and what family he came from, my senior laughed and said, "So, can you just come in through the front? The back is too muddy for people to walk through on most days and we can't have you getting hurt." The local man happily said, "Of course," and I was told to give him a ride back to his friend. He was silent the whole ride back, got out of the vehicle and told his friend that everything was okay. He never came back on the property again, and now I was standing right in front of him as a free man 12 years later.

"I'm so sorry I treated you like that," I said to him in the most genuine and heartfelt way I could. "I was so young and dumb back then, macho, and I gave you no respect."

The local fellow reached down in his cooler and grabbed me one of his delicious concoctions. "Here, take this and relax. All good, braddah, I trust you." I was taken aback as those three words came out of his mouth. *How could this be?* I thought. The complete circumambulation of the situation hit me and I was completely flabbergasted. How did this local man find so much forgiveness in his heart? I learned then and there that throughout the same 12 years we both went through large shifts of maturity. He was indeed angry with me then, but over time had come to grow up and become an adult. I learned that day that just because I had been in a monastery doesn't mean the world stopped when I went in. Everyone had been maturing in one way or another, except for them the teacher had been life itself and not someone as a mentor or teacher figure wearing robes. We all have our own teachers in this life, our own lessons and hardships to experience, and as long as we are observing our experience to be an educational process, then we will learn, evolve and be better.

We will realize that our reactions are under our control, our emotions are guided by our own intelligence, and our actions— or non-actions—are under our guidance as a complete operating system. We are to blame for that which we surround ourselves with, how we react and whatever we feel. The individual is an island all to himself, complete and unstained at this very moment—perfect. Watch carefully in the present moment, reflect on what has come before, and observe how you feel now. You are not determined by anything, you are influenced by some things, everything—your response in the moment and all future moments—is your fault, and nothing will change unless you become the one to change it.

Many years ago, when human civilizations were small and made up of the tribe, we used to have teachers, leaders, role models, fathers and gurus—we used to have masters. In those times we learned from someone much greater than ourselves. That person was more experienced, wiser and able to guide us as we matured. Today, we are born into a society that is guru-less and thus have become lost in a sea of instant distraction. We have skills but no one to help us see them. We have strength but no one to help hone it into wise action. Instead, we are taught to be our own master, our own guru. Left to our own devices, young men and women grow up to lack meaning and purpose. *What am I here for? Where am I going?* Big questions like these shouldn't go unanswered, but should be reflected on within our community. If no one in your tribe has been able to conclude why we are here then may this short answer that I gave to those young men I trained in 2015 suffice:

Responsibility and discipline create purpose. That purpose creates drive. That drive is willpower and creates one victory after another after another. This is self-mastery. This is the path of evolving through challenges. After this challenge is finished a more difficult one will take its place. It must because that is why we are here, to evolve through challenges. When the foundation is built the challenges will get harder but you get stronger. Living like this creates wisdom. Eventually one's own path is no longer as important and helping those who are just starting out becomes the greatest challenge. Changing other people's lives becomes the final goal. All of it is right there inside you the entire time, just like it is inside of me.

BOOKS

SPIRITUALITY

O is a symbol of the world, of oneness and unity; this eye
represents knowledge and insight. We publish titles on general
spirituality and living a spiritual life. We aim to inform and help
you on your own journey in this life.
If you have enjoyed this book, why not tell other readers by
posting a review on your preferred book site?
Recent bestsellers from O-Books are:

Heart of Tantric Sex
Diana Richardson
Revealing Eastern secrets of deep love and intimacy to Western
couples.
Paperback: 978-1-90381-637-0 ebook: 978-1-84694-637-0

Crystal Prescriptions
The A-Z guide to over 1,200 symptoms and their healing crystals
Judy Hall
The first in the popular series of eight books, this handy little
guide is packed as tight as a pill-bottle with crystal remedies for
ailments.
Paperback: 978-1-90504-740-6 ebook: 978-1-84694-629-5

Take Me To Truth
Undoing the Ego
Nouk Sanchez, Tomas Vieira
The best-selling step-by-step book on shedding the Ego, using the teachings of *A Course In Miracles*.
Paperback: 978-1-84694-050-7 ebook: 978-1-84694-654-7

The 7 Myths about Love...Actually!
The Journey from your HEAD to the HEART of your SOUL
Mike George
Smashes all the myths about LOVE.
Paperback: 978-1-84694-288-4 ebook: 978-1-84694-682-0

The Holy Spirit's Interpretation of the New Testament
A Course in Understanding and Acceptance
Regina Dawn Akers
Following on from the strength of *A Course In Miracles*, NTI teaches us how to experience the love and oneness of God.
Paperback: 978-1-84694-085-9 ebook: 978-1-78099-083-5

The Message of A Course In Miracles
A translation of the Text in plain language
Elizabeth A. Cronkhite
A translation of *A Course in Miracles* into plain, everyday language for anyone seeking inner peace. The companion volume, *Practicing A Course In Miracles*, offers practical lessons and mentoring.
Paperback: 978-1-84694-319-5 ebook: 978-1-84694-642-4

Your Simple Path
Find Happiness in every step
Ian Tucker
A guide to helping us reconnect with what is really important in
our lives.
Paperback: 978-1-78279-349-6 ebook: 978-1-78279-348-9

365 Days of Wisdom
Daily Messages To Inspire You Through The Year
Dadi Janki
Daily messages which cool the mind, warm the heart and guide
you along your journey.
Paperback: 978-1-84694-863-3 ebook: 978-1-84694-864-0

Body of Wisdom
Women's Spiritual Power and How it Serves
Hilary Hart
Bringing together the dreams and experiences of women across
the world with today's most visionary spiritual teachers.
Paperback: 978-1-78099-696-7 ebook: 978-1-78099-695-0

Dying to Be Free
From Enforced Secrecy to Near Death to True Transformation
Hannah Robinson
After an unexpected accident and near-death experience, Hannah
Robinson found herself radically transforming her life, while a
remarkable new insight altered her relationship with her father, a
practising Catholic priest.
Paperback: 978-1-78535-254-6 ebook: 978-1-78535-255-3

The Ecology of the Soul
A Manual of Peace, Power and Personal Growth for Real People
in the Real World
Aidan Walker
Balance your own inner Ecology of the Soul to regain your
natural state of peace, power and wellbeing.
Paperback: 978-1-78279-850-7 ebook: 978-1-78279-849-1

Not I, Not other than I
The Life and Teachings of Russel Williams
Steve Taylor, Russel Williams
The miraculous life and inspiring teachings of one of the World's
greatest living Sages.
Paperback: 978-1-78279-729-6 ebook: 978-1-78279-728-9

On the Other Side of Love
A woman's unconventional journey towards wisdom
Muriel Maufroy
When life has lost all meaning, what do you do?
Paperback: 978-1-78535-281-2 ebook: 978-1-78535-282-9

Practicing A Course In Miracles
A translation of the Workbook in plain language, with mentor's
notes
Elizabeth A. Cronkhite
The practical second and third volumes of The Plain-Language
A Course In Miracles.
Paperback: 978-1-84694-403-1 ebook: 978-1-78099-072-9

Quantum Bliss
The Quantum Mechanics of Happiness, Abundance, and Health
George S. Mentz
Quantum Bliss is the breakthrough summary of success and spirituality secrets that customers have been waiting for.
Paperback: 978-1-78535-203-4 ebook: 978-1-78535-204-1

The Upside Down Mountain
Mags MacKean
A must-read for anyone weary of chasing success and happiness – one woman's inspirational journey swapping the uphill slog for the downhill slope.
Paperback: 978-1-78535-171-6 ebook: 978-1-78535-172-3

Your Personal Tuning Fork
The Endocrine System
Deborah Bates
Discover your body's health secret, the endocrine system, and 'twang' your way to sustainable health!
Paperback: 978-1-84694-503-8 ebook: 978-1-78099-697-4

Readers of ebooks can buy or view any of these bestsellers by clicking on the live link in the title. Most titles are published in paperback and as an ebook. Paperbacks are available in traditional bookshops. Both print and ebook formats are available online.

Find more titles and sign up to our readers' newsletter at http://www.johnhuntpublishing.com/mind-body-spirit

Follow us on Facebook at https://www.facebook.com/OBooks/ and Twitter at https://twitter.com/obooks